Justice

A Beginner's Guide

[illegible] d engaging [illegible] ory to religion and poli[illegible] in-between. Innovative and affordable, books in the series are perfect for anyone curious about the way the world works and the big ideas of our time.

aesthetics
africa
american politics
anarchism
ancient philosophy
animal behaviour
anthropology
anti-capitalism
aquinas
archaeology
art
artifi cial intelligence
the baha'i faith
the beat generation
the bible
biodiversity
bioterror & biowarfare
the brain
british politics
the Buddha
cancer
censorship
christianity
civil liberties
classical music
climate change
cloning
the cold war
conservation
crimes against humanity
criminal psychology
critical thinking
the crusades
daoism
democracy
descartes
dewey
dyslexia
economics
energy
engineering
the english civil wars
the enlightenment
epistemology
ethics
the european union
evolution
evolutionary psychology
existentialism
fair trade
feminism
forensic science
french literature
the french revolution
genetics
global terrorism
hinduism
history
the history of medicine
history of science
homer
humanism
huxley
international relations
iran
islamic philosophy
the islamic veil
jazz
journalism
judaism
lacan
life in the universe
literary theory
machiavelli
mafia & organized crime
magic
marx
medieval philosophy
the middle east
modern slavery
NATO
the new testament
nietzsche
nineteenth-century art
the northern ireland confl ict
nutrition
oil
opera
the palestine–israeli confl ict
parapsychology
particle physics
paul
philosophy
philosophy of mind
philosophy of religion
philosophy of science
planet earth
postmodernism
psychology
quantum physics
the qur'an
racism
rawls
reductionism
religion
renaissance art
the roman empire
the russian revolution
shakespeare
shi'i islam
the small arms trade
stalin
sufi sm
the torah
the united nations
the victorians
volcanoes
the world trade organization
war
world war II

Justice

A Beginner's Guide

Raymond Wacks

A Oneworld Paperback Original

Published in North America, Great Britain and Australia by
Oneworld Publications 2017

A CIP record for this title is available from the British Library

ISBN 978-1-78607-045-6

eISBN 978-1-78607-046-3

Typeset by Silicon Chips
Printed and bound in Great Britain by Clays Ltd, St Ives plc

Oneworld Publications
10 Bloomsbury Street
London WC1B 3SR
England

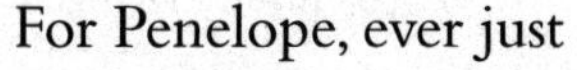

For Penelope, ever just

Contents

Preface ix

1 Justice and injustice 1

2 Justice and virtue 10

3 Rights, dignity and freedom 21

4 Utilitarianism 33

5 Justice as fairness 46

6 Libertarianism 71

7 Capability 82

8 Justice and the free market 95

9 Equality 104

10 Fraternity 121

11 Communitarianism 147

12 Global justice 156

13 Achieving social justice 179

Some key terms 188

Notes and further reading 194

Index 209

Preface

The pursuit of justice is at the heart of social progress. Eliminating the despair and agony of poverty, persecution, disease and inequality is an honourable, if intractable, quest. It requires perseverance, commitment and dedication. Many individuals, groups, charities, domestic and international organizations devote themselves assiduously to relieving the burdens of adversity and suffering.

The question of what constitutes a just society is, however, always contentious. As will be perceived from the pages that follow, there is little consensus on the most desirable social, political and economic arrangements to create a community – or indeed, a world – that might be described as fair.

This book provides an introduction to the manifold theories of justice advanced since antiquity. It attempts to explain, illustrate and compare, as lucidly as possible, the nature, purpose and deficiencies of each of the leading philosophies.

My undertaking was rendered less demanding thanks to the helpful suggestions and advice offered by the anonymous reviewer to whom I am extremely grateful. I am also deeply indebted to Shadi Doostdar of Oneworld, who persuasively admonished me to elucidate and simplify successive drafts of my manuscript. Her extraordinary tenacity, and numerous practical ideas, greatly improved the volume in your hands. My good fortune and gratitude did not end there. Copy editor par excellence, Ann Grand, more than lived up to her name. She detected and corrected my every grammatical infelicity and deftly polished my prose where it fell below her exacting standard.

When we speak of justice, it is well to recall Benjamin Franklin's dictum that 'justice will not be served until those who are unaffected are as outraged as those who are'.

Raymond Wacks

1 Justice and injustice

Imagine a society in which a tiny minority exercises power over a large majority. Let's call the minority the Winners and the majority the Losers. The Winners deny the Losers a variety of important rights, including the right to vote, and they are therefore unrepresented in parliament. They may not live where they choose and the best jobs are denied them by law. Their homes, schools and hospitals are inferior to those provided for the Winners. Sexual relations and marriage between the Winners and Losers are prohibited by the criminal law and punishable by imprisonment. The Losers must carry identity documents at all times and are subject to a curfew at night.

Could such a society exist? Is injustice on this scale possible?

It did. And it was. I was born and grew up in this society. Under the system of apartheid, the white minority of South Africa reserved the most fundamental rights and privileges for itself. So-called 'non-whites' were considered inferior and were subjugated and oppressed, while the minority maintained a masquerade of parliamentary democracy – but only for the whites.

The legal system was the creation of that minority; the political system disenfranchised all non-white people and the law discriminated against them in almost every facet of social and economic life: employment, land, housing, education, even sex.

Their freedom of movement was ruthlessly curtailed. Deaths in detention and torture were systemic. Surveillance, intimidation and police brutality were routine. Apartheid South Africa was the very model of a modern police state. The *Broederbond*, a formidably powerful, secret, Calvinist, all-male society, fostered Afrikaner interests and white racial superiority. Every prime minister and state president throughout the apartheid era (1948–1994) was a member, including the architect of the policy, Hendrik Verwoerd, who famously declared that the role of his government was 'the preservation of the white man and his state'. Under his premiership, apartheid was not only consolidated, but also clothed in philosophical, cultural and theological validation that drew on the seductive power of Afrikaner nationalism.

Apartheid, it is frequently forgotten, was not merely racial segregation. It was an elaborate, intricate project, sustained by a doctrinaire policy applied by a totalitarian regime bolstered by draconian legislation. It relied on an unaccountable security force holding sweeping powers and a largely enthusiastic legislature and mostly pliant judiciary whose jurisdiction over matters pertaining to human rights was severely limited.

'Anti-terrorism' legislation was skilfully crafted to stifle political opposition. The breadth of the Suppression of Communism Act of 1950 was equalled by the Terrorism Act of 1967, which defined 'terrorism' to include anything that might 'endanger the maintenance of law and order'. Life sentences in South Africa were exactly that. And the gallows were kept busy: between 1910 and 1989 more than 4,200 executions were carried out. About half of those hanged met their end between 1978 and 1989, when the struggle against apartheid was at its peak. The overwhelming majority of those put to death were black; many were political prisoners. At the end of July 1989, for example, 283 prisoners were being held on death row at Pretoria Central Prison. Of these, 272 were black, eleven were white. In March 1988, fifty-three people were hanged for politically related crimes.

On arrival in the country, any white-skinned foreigner with no connection to South Africa and the appropriate visas was instantly entitled to most of the privileges denied to blacks, whose links went back centuries. The white foreigner would be free to choose schools, universities and homes and could enjoy a range of public and private facilities – hospitals, housing, cinemas and theatres – reserved for whites.

Injustice in our world is pervasive. But the abomination of apartheid was especially inhuman. In 1973, the United Nations sought to crystallize apartheid's essence by establishing it as a crime. According to the Apartheid Convention, the offence consists of inhuman acts committed for the purpose of maintaining domination by one racial group over any other and systematically oppressing them. The drafter, in pursuit of greater precision, provides a catalogue of the acts that are embraced by the crime, including murder, torture, inhuman treatment and arbitrary arrest of members of a racial group, legislation that discriminates in the political, social, economic and cultural fields, separate residential areas for racial groups, the prohibition of interracial marriages and the persecution of opponents of apartheid.

The text of the convention captures the quintessential elements of apartheid as applied in South Africa, even though it drains it of much of the system's malevolence and authoritarianism. And, despite the demise of apartheid in 1994, the offence lives on. The Rome Statute of the International Criminal Court (ICC) which came into effect in 2002, included apartheid, along with a catalogue of other wrongs such as murder, extermination, enslavement and torture, as a crime against humanity. The 'crime of apartheid' is defined as 'inhumane acts … committed in the context of an institutionalized regime of systematic oppression and domination by one racial group over any other racial group or groups and committed with the intention of maintaining that regime'.

Figure 1: The author with Nelson Mandela in 1991 after Mandela's release from 27 years' imprisonment.

The experience of living in South Africa during the dark years of apartheid had a profound effect on my political outlook. From an early age I was unable to comprehend how a community could subject fellow humans to the misery, humiliation and poverty on which the system was built. Yet most whites had little difficulty in rationalizing this cruelty. The bastions of this unjust society, of course, came crashing down with the freeing of Nelson Mandela and the establishment of a democratic non-racial constitution in 1994.

Apartheid is an extreme example of injustice. It imposed not only racial inequality but the denial of the most basic rights to non-whites. Although blacks constituted some seventy percent of the population, they were restricted to about thirteen percent of the land. The system of 'influx control' restricted their entry into 'white areas', save as itinerant workers.

These are merely the rudiments of an unjust society that was universally stigmatized as wicked and heartless. But its features provide a template by which we can recognize the central elements of injustice and so seek to identify the components of a *just* society. Can we work backwards like Aristotle and, by constructing a model of a fair society, endeavour to avoid an *unjust* one? Does this assist our quest for a compelling theory of social justice that is the principal purpose of this book?

Consider some of the characteristics of apartheid South Africa. If you turn the denial of rights, interests or values on its head, you will gain a sense of what *positive* principles drive the theories discussed in the pages that follow. For example, racial discrimination is the very opposite of equality. The humiliation of its victims deprives them of human dignity; their exclusion from political participation is a fundamental denial of civil liberties; the inequitable distribution of resources is unfair; the poverty caused by inequality thwarts human flourishing; and so on.

Look around. There is little evidence of justice in our world. War, hunger, exploitation, environmental despoliation, corruption, racism, sexism, disease and poverty seem endemic. Forty percent of our planet's population – three billion people – exists in dire poverty, earning less than US$2 per day. The gap between the rich north and the poor south continues to grow. The average per capita gross domestic product in the north is almost twenty times that of the south. A quarter of the world's population enjoys the fruits of wealth and consumerism as it exploits eighty percent of the earth's resources. In developing countries, one person in five goes hungry every day. Two out of three lack safe drinking water. Illiteracy and unemployment are rife. A quarter of adult men and half the women of the south are illiterate. One child in six is born underweight. Every year one child in ten dies from water-borne diseases or malnutrition. Women constitute seventy percent of the world's poor and, in much of the south, they work harder but earn less than men; they are more likely to be undernourished as a consequence of discrimination in the allocation of food.

Discrimination on the grounds of race, sex, religion and belief continue to be an intractable impediment on the path towards justice. The enormous inequalities in wealth between rich and poor countries create the need for 'global justice' that extends beyond individual states to the world at large. The statistics are disturbing and distressing. It is astonishing to think that, according to the World Health Organization (WHO), about 2.4 billion people – half the developing world – do not have access to toilets and 1.8 billion people are forced to drink water contaminated with faeces. As a result, 1.6 million people die every year from diarrhoeal diseases (including cholera) attributable to lack of access to safe drinking water and basic sanitation. Ninety percent of these are children under five, mostly in developing countries.

Almost a billion people lack adequate shelter and 1.6 billion have no electricity. There are 218 million child labourers. It is inexcusable that in the twenty-first century, one-third of deaths – eighteen million every year – is due to poverty-related causes that are easily preventable through improved nutrition, clean drinking water, vaccines, antibiotics and other medicine.

Although there are signs that progress is being made, famine, environmental degradation, disease (including the devastation wrought by AIDS), deforestation, natural disasters and war are pervasive in developing countries. The effects of climate change were recently described as one of the gravest threats facing the planet. But there is growing anger and impatience across the world about the injustices of the widening gap between rich and poor, government corruption, the huge bonuses paid to bankers and the general tardiness in palpable progress towards greater fairness. The resentment sporadically spills over into protests, occasionally violent, in many parts of the world. The Occupy movement, for example, is a conspicuous global crusade against social and economic inequality. It pursues greater equity in the distribution of wealth with a particular emphasis on the negative impact of the international financial system on democracy and justice.

The concept of justice clearly requires some model to which societies can aspire. It requires a theory. Every society is organized according to some theory of justice, whether express or implied. A recurring theme in theories of justice is the conflict between the rights of individuals to live the lives they choose, on the one hand, and the right or duty of the community to interfere with this autonomy for one reason or another, on the other. Justice – or 'social justice' as it is often called – is not merely the absence of injustice. Any theory of justice includes ideas about how society and its laws should be arranged, what is best for both individuals and the community and how the legitimate ambitions of people can best be realized.

Social justice

The idea of justice is employed in numerous disciplines, mainly in philosophy but also law, politics, sociology and gender studies, to mention a few. Our principal concern in these pages is with 'social justice', whose main focus is on how to create a fair relationship between society and the individual. In particular, it looks to the distribution of wealth and opportunity and how people can best exercise and develop their roles in, and expectations of, society. It calls for a number of factors, including taxation, education, medical services and the regulation of markets to be established in order to arrive at a more just social order.

Any theory of justice must confront the recurring question of how goods are to be distributed in society. Co-operation is at the heart of any community. Humans are not hermits; we interact socially and economically to our mutual advantage. Principles of distribution should specify how the benefits and burdens are to be allocated. Theories differ as to how this should be done.

Egalitarians argue that everyone should get an equal slice of the pie. Utilitarians favour increasing the overall happiness or welfare of the community. Rawlsians prefer the adoption of the difference principle, which ensures that the least well-off are protected. Libertarians oppose any set (or what they call 'patterned') distribution and support the right of people to own what they have legitimately acquired. Desert-based theories of justice advocate the idea that people should get what they deserve as a result, for example, of their hard work or need. These theories – and a number of others – are the main subject of this book.

RIGHT AND WRONG

Nelson Mandela: 'Our human compassion binds us the one to the other – not in pity or patronizingly but as human beings who have learnt how to turn our common suffering into hope for the future.'

Sophocles: 'The golden eye of justice sees and requites the unjust man.'

Joseph Conrad: 'The conquest of the earth, which mostly means the taking it away from those who have a different complexion or slightly flatter noses than ourselves, is not a pretty thing when you look into it too much. What redeems it is the idea only. An idea at the back of it; not a sentimental pretence but an idea; and an unselfish belief in the idea – something you can set up and bow down before and offer a sacrifice to.'

Aristotle: 'All virtue is summed up in dealing justly.'

Heraclitus: 'If it were not for injustice, men would not know justice.'

Edmund Burke: 'What is the use of discussing a man's abstract right to food or medicine? The question is upon the method of procuring and administering them. In that deliberation I shall always advise to call in the aid of the farmer and the physician rather than the professor of metaphysics.'

Montesquieu: 'There is no greater tyranny than that which is perpetrated under the shield of the law and in the name of justice.'

Samuel Johnson: 'Justice is my being allowed to do whatever I like. Injustice is whatever prevents my doing so.'

Any fully developed theory of justice must articulate and justify how to organize a community according to circumstances that are morally appropriate. The emphasis of today's many social justice movements is on the injustices they perceive to be a consequence of capitalism and the means by which the least advantaged might be protected from the system's worst excesses.

Consider your country. Is the gap between the rich and the poor widening or closing? Do women have equal rights to men? What about the disabled, the LGBT community, other minorities? Are they denied the opportunities that are afforded to the able-bodied? Is the welfare of animals adequately protected? If you had the power to decide how your society could be made more just, what principles would you adopt? A free market economy? One in which justice is measured by what created the greatest happiness for the majority? Or perhaps a society in which everyone has equal opportunities or equal pay? These, as we shall see, are merely some of the possible models you might want to adopt.

Each of the following chapters attempts to illuminate the central features of the leading conceptions of justice. This is not to say that each is discrete; there is an inevitable degree of overlap. My purpose is to enable you to see the main approaches to this elusive ideal.

What follows is, I hope, a voyage of discovery; a voyage not merely of academic but of practical importance in our endeavour to secure a just society and a better world.

2 Justice and virtue

The British philosopher, Alfred Whitehead (1867–1941), famously remarked that the development of Western philosophy is a series of footnotes to Plato. Despite the passage of thousands of years, the starting-point of any discussion of justice is the writing of the great Greek philosophers. Plato (c. 424–348 BCE) was disenchanted with the state of affairs in Athens – especially its extreme individualism – and presents an elaborate model of an ideal society in which justice is paramount. In his book, *Republic,* he describes it as a 'human virtue' that secures order and generates both individual goodness and social harmony.

Plato's pupil, Aristotle (384–322 BCE) advances a less comprehensive account of justice that remains highly influential. In his book, *Nicomachean Ethics,* he probes deeply into the moral and political virtue of justice, and in his book, *Politics*, he examines the relationship between political justice and equality. But his approach, like that of Plato, is not what we would today describe as egalitarian (that is, based on equality). Justice, he argues, means equality *only for those who are equals*. Agreeing with Plato that political democracy is inherently unjust because it seeks to treat unequals as if they were equals, justice, he claims, requires *inequality* for those who are *unequal*.

His analysis of equality is part of a much broader and more intricate account of humanity and politics. He differentiates between numerical and proportional equality. In the first, everyone is treated as indistinguishable; they receive identical treatment in respect of the goods they receive. The second, proportional equality, arises when the goods people obtain are proportional or roughly equal to what they are considered to be entitled to. Numerical equality is fair only when people are equal in *relevant respects*. This means that while we can and should aspire to treating people equally, it is clear that we cannot *make* everyone equal, since everyone is different. For example, no two stones are exactly equal; they are different in weight, shape and colour. Similarly, in the case of living creatures, each individual is unique. For many years I kept chickens (strongly recommended), and it soon became evident that every hen has her own personality and character. Likewise, we humans differ markedly in our talents, abilities and appearances.

To attempt to make us all equal would be to reduce the most able to the level of the least. Giving every person an *equal opportunity*, though difficult, is vital, but some people will be lucky, or work harder and achieve more. But we are equal in relevant respects: for example, we all have feelings, needs and desires. Proportional equality is more detailed: it sets out a complete formulation of formal equality, a matter to be discussed in Chapter 9. As we shall see, all disagreements about the ideal theory of justice – that is, who is entitled to what – turn on the central question of which cases are regarded as equal and which are considered unequal.

Aristotle's important claim is that justice consists of treating equals equally and 'unequals' unequally, in proportion to their inequality: everyone must be treated in such a way that the outcome is equal for them. People who for whatever reason are considered equals must receive the same degree of respect. For example, suppose Boris and Doris both teach history at the same school to pupils at the same level. Since there are no relevant differences between them or their occupation, they should receive the same salary. If Boris is paid more than Doris merely because he is a man or because he is white, this would be unjust. Doris would be a victim of discrimination on the grounds of her sex or race, neither of which are relevant.

It is worth reflecting for a moment on a general question that is touched on in many of the theories discussed in this book. It is often thought that in democratic societies there is an unavoidable conflict between liberty and equality. This view is based on the idea that liberty or freedom to do as one pleases (provided it does not affect someone else's liberty), is restricted by attempts to create equality between individuals, that in a truly free society the government should resist introducing measures that seek to make people equal by, for example, redistributing wealth. Libertarians, in their defence of the free market, generally oppose any redistribution by means of taxation, which promotes equality (as will become clear in Chapter 6). But some doubt whether liberty is incompatible or in conflict with equality. Ronald Dworkin, for example, contends that there is no necessary conflict. This is because a genuine restriction on liberty occurs only when it affects someone who has done nothing wrong. It is perfectly legitimate for the state to curtail my liberty, for example, by enacting laws against murder or rape. But when no wrong has been committed, liberty is not restricted by measures to advance equality. We will return to this question in Chapter 9.

Aristotle's approach to equality reveals a rather hierarchical view. To him, women and non-Greeks were inferior to male Greeks. His strong belief in their inequality led him to assert that 'inferiors' ought to be deprived of certain political, legal, social and economic rights. He therefore fails to respect all individuals as rational and free. This concentration on *inequality* results in his failure to recognise the moral equality of all. Aristotle also distinguishes between *corrective* justice on the one hand and *distributive* justice on the other. Corrective justice is, in his opinion, the justice the courts employ to redress crimes or civil wrongs. It is an attempt to put things back in the position they were. For example, a court may award an injured party pecuniary damages (that is, money) to compensate for pain and suffering. Corrective justice requires that all must be treated equally.

This is closely connected to *retributive* justice (which Aristotle does not consider in any detail). The general purpose of retributive justice is to impose a proportionate punishment on those who commit crimes. It is based on the moral idea that wrongdoers *deserve* to be punished for their crime because it is just that they should be. Distributive justice has a similar objective: it seeks to give to each person according to his desert or merit. It emphasises fairness in what people receive, especially goods; it is sometimes called 'economic justice' for that reason. Distributive justice, in Aristotle's view, should be left to the legislature. Such distribution will depend on the nature of the government in question; a capitalist society will distribute wealth differently from a socialist one.

Aristotle also proposes an important theory of how we ought to live. Following Plato, he regards the *ethical virtues* (including justice, temperance and courage) as rational, emotional and social skills. If we are to live well, we must grasp how values such as friendship, pleasure, virtue, wealth and honour form a coherent whole. By learning general rules, we develop the practical wisdom to behave in the most rational way. We also require emotional and social skills to put into practice our general understanding of well-being.

Central to his discussion of virtue is the quest for the 'Golden Mean'. If justice is a virtue, he argues, it must be a kind of mean: a halfway point between the two extremes of excess and deficiency. The virtue of courage – if present in excess – becomes recklessness and, if deficient, it takes the form of cowardice. Our lives are replete with moral dilemmas. But there is no *single rule* that we can apply to them all. Our obligations cannot be frozen in a code that is all-encompassing. This is the core of the 'doctrine of the mean'. Aristotelian virtue ethics thus escapes the uncompromising forms of duty embraced by both philosophers who base their theories on duty (deontologists), such as Immanuel Kant, and those who base them on outcomes (consequentialists), such as Jeremy Bentham (discussed in Chapters 3 and 4).

Aristotle stresses the importance of both character and virtue. Character is a state of being: if I am a kind person I have the right *feelings* toward others. But our character or inner temperament also dictates our *action*. This differs from the approaches of deontology and consequentialism, which are more concerned with *right action*. The virtue ethics approach associated with Aristotle looks to the question of *what constitutes a good life* and what kind of person we ought to be. It is, therefore *character*-based.

There is no absolute precision to be found in Aristotle's concept of justice. Instead, he attempts to identify the key characteristics of *injustice* and works backwards from there to comprehend the elements of justice. This is similar to the method we employ when we try to define what constitutes a healthy person: we know when someone is *unhealthy* and are thus able to identify its opposite. An individual who is greedy or who disobeys the law is unjust, whereas one who obeys the law and seeks only his fair share is just.

Political animals

Aristotle's notion of justice is related to his general theory of constitutionalism and citizenship. The politician, he writes, 'is wholly occupied with the city-state and the constitution is a certain way of organizing those who inhabit the city-state'. In Athens, he distinguishes citizens from other inhabitants, including, in his words, 'resident aliens', people we would today call immigrants and slaves. A citizen is defined as one who has the right to participate in political or judicial office. The constitution is the means by which to arrange the offices of the city-state, principally the office of sovereign or ruler. The constitution therefore determines what constitutes the governing body, which may take different forms depending on the nature of the state: in a democracy it is the people; in an oligarchy it is a select few (the affluent or well-born).

We are by nature, Aristotle contends, political animals who want to live together. He differentiates the forms of rule by which one individual or group can rule over another. First there is *despotic rule*, which is typified by the master-slave relationship. He – surprisingly – justifies slavery by asserting that natural-born slaves lack the ability to make purposeful decisions and therefore need a master to direct them. Second, he identifies *paternal* and *marital rules*, claiming that men (as opposed to women) and senior members of society possess a natural capacity for leadership.

Such paternalism jars with contemporary views on equality, but for Aristotle, children and wives are to be looked after, just as doctors look after patients. He argues that paternal and marital rules are applied in the interest of the child and wife in the same way as medicine is pursued for the sake of the patient. In this sense they are similar to political rule, which is the form of rule suitable when the ruler and the subject have equal or comparable rational capacities. This is illustrated by naturally equal citizens taking turns at ruling for one another's advantage. This leads him to conclude that constitutions that advance the common benefit are perfectly just, while those that seek only to benefit the rulers are unjust, because they entail despotic rule, which is wrong for a community of free people. Drawing on this analysis, he identifies six possible constitutional arrangements (see Table 1).

Table 1

	Just	**Deviant**
One ruler	Kingship	Tyranny
Few rulers	Aristocracy	Oligarchy
Many rulers	Polity	Democracy

This is where Aristotle's understanding of justice takes off. He argues that democracy (where the dominant class tends to be the poor) is preferable to an oligarchy (which is normally composed of the wealthy members of the community). But 'polity' (which is a combination of oligarchy and democracy) is a system of rule that involves a mix between the moderately rich and the poor. The purpose of political life is to create virtuous citizens and promote goodness in individuals. According to Aristotle any *polis* (or city-state):

> … which is truly so called and is not merely one in name must devote itself to the end of encouraging goodness. Otherwise a political association sinks into a mere 'alliance' and the law 'becomes a mere covenant' that guarantees men's rights against one another instead of being 'a rule of life such as will make the members of a polis good and just'.

This means that politics should not only be concerned with majority rule or protecting individual rights, but also with promoting the skills required to live a virtuous life: practical judgement, participation in the exercise of democratic government and concern for the well-being of the community.

Democracy: the least worst system

The worst regime, argues Aristotle, is tyranny; democracy is the least worst. Democratic rule is not merely the rule of the multitude, since in every regime the majority has authority. The difference between democracy and oligarchy is that democracy exists when the free and the poor, being a majority, have the authority to rule. Oligarchy, on the other hand, is where a minority – the wealthy and 'better born' – exercise authority. But there are several types of democracy. The first is based mainly on equality, where the poor and the well-off are treated equally and the majority govern since both groups have equal authority to do so.

Regimes and cities consist of three sections: the very wealthy, the very poor and those in the middle. Since the mean is always the most desirable, the middling element of the city (what we would call the 'middle class') is the best part. This accords with Aristotle's general view that virtue is a mean between two extremes of vice. A sizeable middle class is, he argues, vital for a stable and well-run government because the middle class does not hanker after power, it lacks envy and, because its members share similar values, they form attachments. Its members are therefore able to act as neutral mediators between rich and poor. Located between the wealthy (whom they dislike) and the deprived (whom they fear), they are more likely to be reasonable and help maintain a stable community. Aristotle acknowledges that this ideal exists only in theory, but by reflecting on it and attempting to describe its laws, structure and core principles, we can arrive at a model against which to judge other regimes to determine which is the most appropriate.

Impartiality or neutrality is a significant element in most theories of justice. You will find it depicted in material form as Themis, the goddess of justice and law, who typically clutches a sword in one hand and a pair of scales in the other. The sword represents the power of the judge, while the scales symbolize the balance and discernment with which justice is carried out. Artists in the sixteenth century portrayed her blindfolded, to underline that justice is blind: resistant to pressure and influence. A fine example can be found in the statue above the Central Criminal Court (the 'Old Bailey') in London.

Doing the right thing

Let's stop for a moment and consider how this might work in practice. A popular hypothetical example is to suppose that a known terrorist has planted a nuclear bomb that is set to detonate within a few hours. He refuses to disclose its location. Should we torture him to persuade him to disclose the whereabouts of the bomb? Would it be morally wrong *not* to torture him, to save the lives of thousands? Is torturing a single individual justified to protect the many?

Our dilemma boils down to whether one adopts a deontological or consequential moral position. Deontology holds that certain acts are *intrinsically* right or wrong, regardless of their consequences; the moral worth of an action is logically independent of its outcome: 'Let justice be done though the heavens fall!' is one of its lofty maxims. Consequentialism is its opposite: it looks to the consequences of an act or rule to determine its moral value. Thus a deontologist would regard torture as *always* wrong, while a consequentialist is likely to defend torture where it is the only practical means by which *to prevent greater harm*.

This hypothetical situation illuminates how – when it comes to formulating an acceptable theory of justice – one's philosophical starting-point is key. To put it crudely, Kant would say no to torture; Bentham, yes. The basis of these contrasting positions will become clear in a moment.

Answering Aristotle

Aristotle was more interested in *good* action than *right* action. For him, the purpose (*telos*), of social and political associations is to promote good action. He held man's virtue above any other social distinction or hierarchy, such as wealth or descent:

> Those who contribute most to an association of this character, i.e. who contribute most to good action, have a greater share in the polis and should therefore, in justice, receive a larger recognition from it than those who are equal to them (or even greater) in free birth and descent but unequal in civic excellence or than those who surpass them in wealth but are, surpassed by them in excellence.

You may think that our political leaders could usefully be replaced by those who exhibit these virtues! They deserve this honour, according to Aristotle, because of their civic virtue and leadership skills. This may strike you as a rather utopian vision, far removed from the shenanigans, intrigue, compromise and greed that frequently characterize the politics of today. Yet Aristotle believes that it is only through politics that we achieve and express our complete human nature. We are designed for political engagement, since we have the capacity for language that enables us to articulate, debate and distinguish between good and bad, just and unjust. By exercising these abilities we learn how to become virtuous: 'Moral excellence comes about as a result of habit. We become just by doing just acts, temperate by doing temperate acts, brave by doing brave acts'.

What about his justification of slavery? Surely this is an institution of quintessential inequality. Our contemporary sensibilities are, of course, profoundly opposed to any form of slavery but it was a fundamental characteristic of the Athenian state. Nevertheless, for Aristotle to offer a defence of slavery based on his concept of justice seems peculiar. However, justice, in Aristotle's view, is a question of fit: it is about allowing individuals to realize their true nature. For slavery to be just, not only must it be necessary, it should also be natural. It is natural because certain individuals are intended, by their nature, to become slaves. Its necessity springs, he says, from the freedom it affords citizens to participate in political life because their slaves attend to menial tasks at home. Where, however, free men have been forced into slavery (for example as prisoners of war), their slavery is unjust. Where a slave is not naturally predisposed to his predicament, his master has no right to compel him to continue his enslavement. Still, it seems difficult to accept Aristotle's defence unless you also accept Aristotle's notion of 'justice as fit'.

Summing up

Is justice consistent with the sort of inequality that Aristotle defends? Can a just society permit slavery and sexual inequality? Aristotle is in no doubt that those who are intellectually and morally inferior are rightly treated as political and social inferiors in a properly ordered *polis*. He argues that certain individuals are naturally superior and therefore fit to rule, while others are naturally inferior and suited to be ruled by others. Men, he asserts, are naturally superior to women and hence fit to rule. Indeed, it is in their own interests that women are ruled by men in the same way that 'natural slaves' are ruled by the 'naturally free'.

In this respect his account of justice fails to respect all individuals as rational free agents. By concentrating on the manner in which people are *un*equal, his theory is difficult to accept in our modern age of equality and human rights.

3

Rights, dignity and freedom

The philosopher Immanuel Kant (1724–1804), was a creature of habit. Born in the Prussian city of Königsberg (he couldn't be more different from Woody Allen), he would, on rising, drink a cup or two of weak tea, smoke his pipe and prepare his lectures, which he would deliver from seven until eleven in the morning. He continued writing until lunch, after which he would religiously set out on his daily walk and spend the rest of the afternoon with his English friend, Joseph Green. His neighbours reputedly set their watches by the moment Kant emerged from their meeting. After returning home, he would undertake a little light work, read and then, presumably, sleep.

For Kant, justice is intimately bound up with duty. To say that we have duties of justice to other people is to say that they have rights against us. Basing justice on duty means that Kant regards what is *right* as independent of what we consider to be *good*. Justice requires respect for the right, regardless of difficult circumstances and desirable and undesirable consequences. People have the right to be respected as individuals, *as ends in themselves*.

The *priority of right*, according to Kant, arises from the freedom that individuals have in their relationships; it has nothing to do with achieving happiness. Justice and right come before all other values because they stem from the idea of *freedom* which, in turn, is a prerequisite of all human ends.

Kant's austere, ascetic character emerges from his often turgid but hugely influential writings. In his famous work, *Groundwork for the Metaphysics of Morals*, he develops his strict, deontological (duty-based) view of morality, claiming: 'A good will is good not because of what it effects or accomplishes, nor because of its fitness to attain some proposed end; it is good only through its willing, i.e., it is good in itself'. What he means is that good will underlies moral worth, which turns not on our particular conduct but on the *principle upon which the act is done.*

This test imposes stringent obligations; we all lie. Recently a friend asked me whether she looked good in her new, expensive pair of jeans. She looked terrible. I could not bring myself to tell her the truth, so I uttered a 'white lie' attesting to her attractiveness in the trousers. I did not want to hurt her feelings. Did I behave immorally? Kant would say yes. Lying, according to him, is always wrong, regardless of its effects.

Kant's absolutist prohibition of lying flows from his view that when I lie I extinguish my human dignity. I am reduced to nothing more than a thing. This inflexibility extends to the classic case in which a would-be murderer asks you whether 'our friend who is pursued by him had taken refuge in your house'. Surely you would want to lie to protect the probable victim? What if, for example, a suspicious SS officer in pursuit of Jews to transport to a concentration camp had quizzed a German who knew where a Jewish family was hiding? And what of the guilt of the German when the family was apprehended and sent to their its death? Kant seeks to mitigate this guilt by claiming that by being truthful you cannot be held responsible for the evil acts of another. In telling the truth, the German has not acted immorally. If, however, he lies, he becomes responsible for the immoral consequences that might transpire. Similarly, for Kant, torture is always wrong, notwithstanding that it might produce useful information from the victim that could save lives.

Kant's imperatives

The duty not to lie is an example of a negative duty. In addition to these negative duties, Kant adds positive obligations to assist those in danger. He seeks to formulate a concept of right that is independent of our practical desires, interests and needs. To do so, he states that we must have a single fundamental principle of duty, which he calls the '*categorical imperative*'. It informs us of what we ought to do categorically (by which he means unconditionally) and enables us rationally to distinguish between right and wrong. It comes in three different forms:

1. A formula of *universalizability*: we must attempt to do only what we could reasonably want to become a universal law.
2. A prescription for *respect for all persons*: we should always try to act in such a way as to respect all persons, including ourselves, as innately valuable 'ends in themselves' and never treat any persons merely as instrumental means to other ends.
3. A *'principle of autonomy'*: we, as morally autonomous rational agents, should try to act in such a way that we could be legislating for a (hypothetical) moral republic of all persons. This principle stresses the dignity of all persons, treating them as intrinsically valuable and worthy of respect.

The only legitimate reason for acting morally, Kant insists, is that you are under a *duty* to do so. This is very important. If you act from some *other* motive (for instance, fear of punishment) you are not acting *morally*. Suppose you purchased this book to impress your friends. You have no intention of reading it but by pretending to, you hope to create the impression that you are a serious person. You have acquired the book merely to achieve a purpose that Kant calls *heteronomous* (acting in accordance with your *desires* rather than reason or moral duty) as opposed to *autonomous* (based on your own personal *morality*). You are not acting morally; you have an ulterior motive.

From this example we may develop Kant's defence of what it is to be a moral person. The value of our conduct lies in the *intention or motive* with which it is executed. Its moral worth lies not in the consequences of an action but in the act itself: doing the right thing for the right reason. In contrast, when we seek to fulfil our desires, we act from self-interest. Acting morally requires us to act out of *duty*.

When I act in accordance with these categorical imperatives, I am required to treat people with *respect*. I treat them not in pursuit of some secondary or ulterior motive but as *ends in themselves*. And when I do so, I am acting freely. I do not act freely when I act to satisfy an end unconnected to myself for some other motive. In such circumstances my freedom is diminished, since my purpose is to achieve some external objective. Only by acting autonomously rather than in response to circumstances am I free.

The key to understanding Kant's moral philosophy is the requirement that people are treated as ends, not merely as means to some other end. As rational beings, we have *dignity*. This is why Kant condemns suicide; to kill oneself is to 'sink lower than the beasts … Nothing more terrible can be imagined'. Moreover, suicide debases our humanity. Whether or not this is a compelling argument, it highlights the significance Kant attaches both to self-respect and respect for others. Here is the mainspring of the concept of human rights and its central place in the idea of justice and of freedom and the reason Kant spurns the utilitarian approach to justice. It measures justice by reference to a calculation of whether most people benefit from a particular act or policy. It therefore treats people as a *means* to a particular end, and it also requires a community to approve a particular model of happiness. This entails foisting one concept of pleasure on everyone and fails to respect the right of every individual to follow his own lights.

No less uncompromising is Kant's attitude towards retribution:

> Even if a civil society were to be dissolved by the consent of all its members (e.g., if a people inhabiting an island decided to separate and disperse throughout the world), the last murderer remaining in prison would first have to be executed, so that each has done to him what his deeds deserve and blood guilt does not cling to the people for not having insisted upon this punishment; for otherwise the people can be regarded as collaborators in his public violation of justice.

Kant's moral universe is, as we have seen, governed by the notion that we are rational agents who know what we are doing and hence may legitimately be held responsible for our actions. Our rational nature means that we accept the categorical imperative: what applies to me should apply to all; you may treat me as I treat you. If I am kind to others, I approve of their being kind to me. If I exploit them, I consent to the same mistreatment. My deceit invites punishment; I have brought it on myself. Kant's moral theory recognizes not only the offender's state of mind but also the standard to be applied in fixing moral responsibility and a rationale for punishing breaches of those standards.

Liberty, rights and human rights

Many of the dominant themes first expressed in Kant's moral philosophy remain influential in current justifications of human rights, especially the ideals of equality and the moral autonomy of rational human beings. Kant's legacy to our contemporary understanding and defence of human rights is the notion of a community of rational individuals autonomously determining the moral principles to establish the conditions for equality and autonomy. He offers means by which to justify human rights as the foundation for self-determination based on human reason. The philosopher Isaiah Berlin (1909–1997) famously distinguished between 'positive' and 'negative' liberty. Positive liberty includes the role each of us has to play in our government; negative liberty refers to the part of our lives that should be free of government interference. Both deploy the language of rights.

The three approaches that might be adopted are *right-based, duty-based and goal-based.* This (often elusive) difference is illuminated by the philosopher Jeremy Waldron: if our opposition to torture is based on the suffering of the victim, our approach is *right*-based. If we consider that torture demeans the torturer, our concern is *duty*-based. If we regard torture as offensive only when it affects the interests of those other than the torturer and victim, our approach is utilitarian *goal*-based.

Rights are unquestionably fashionable. They are marshalled in support of almost any claim that individuals or groups wish to enjoy. Although the concept, in the form of 'natural rights', first appeared in the Middle Ages, the recognition in the seventeenth and eighteenth centuries of the secular notion of human rights was an historic intellectual moment. It is founded on the idea that such rights are not 'given' by state or government but are fundamental and inalienable, regardless of whether they are legally recognized. Following the horrors of the Holocaust, the Universal Declaration of Human Rights was adopted in 1948. It protects a wide variety of rights, including traditional civil and political rights, the right to life, liberty and security of person; freedom from slavery and servitude; freedom from torture or cruel, inhuman or degrading treatment or punishment; equality before the law and equal protection of the law; freedom from arbitrary arrest, detention or exile; the right to be presumed innocent until proved guilty; the right to protection against arbitrary interference with one's privacy, family, home or correspondence and to protection against attacks upon one's honour and reputation; freedom of movement and residence; the right to leave any country, including one's own; the right to seek and enjoy in other countries asylum from persecution; the right to a nationality and the right to change one's nationality; the right of men and women of full age to marry, without any limitation due to race, nationality or religion; freedom of thought, conscience and religion; the right to own property and not to be deprived of it arbitrarily; freedom of opinion and expression; the right to peaceful assembly and association; the right to take part in the government of one's country; and the right to equal access to public service. Economic and social rights, including the right to social security, are also protected.

Along with the International Covenants on Civil and Political Rights and Economic, Social and Cultural Rights in 1976, these agreements exhibit a dedication by nations to the universal

THE INTERNATIONAL BILL OF HUMAN RIGHTS

In June 1946 the United Nations established the Commission on Human Rights which, under the chairmanship of Eleanor Roosevelt, drafted the text that was adopted on 10 December 1948 by the UN General Assembly (South Africa, conspicuously, was among the eight countries that abstained from voting, to safeguard its system of apartheid).

The declaration represents the first international expression of the notion that every person is inherently entitled to certain human rights. It contains thirty articles that, whilst not legally binding, have been expanded in successive international treaties, regional instruments and domestic constitutions. The International Bill of Human Rights, which incorporated the declaration, was ratified by the UN in 1976, granting it the (limited) force of international law. It was hailed as 'a veritable *Magna Carta* marking mankind's arrival at a vitally important phase: the conscious acquisition of human dignity and worth'. Human Rights Day is celebrated across the globe every year on 10 December.

conception and protection of human rights. The law of many nations now protects human rights through a variety of legislative, judicial and constitutional means. Bills of rights have become a key feature of modern democracies.

The nature and content of human rights have changed over time. The first generation consisted of mostly negative civil and political rights. There then followed a series of fundamentally positive economic, social and cultural rights. The third generation rights are chiefly collective, presaged in Article 28 of the Universal Declaration, which declares that 'everyone is entitled to a social and international order in which the rights set forth in this Declaration can be fully realized'. These so-called 'solidarity' rights include the right to social and economic development, the right to participate in and benefit from the resources of the earth and space, the right to scientific and technical information (which are especially important to the Third World) and the right to a healthy environment, peace and humanitarian disaster relief.

As they are conceived to be 'universal', human rights are more fundamental than ordinary political rights. Indeed, such is their standing that a breach may validate international intervention. There has been a number of incidents where violations of human rights in the Middle East and Africa have resulted in United Nations sanctions being imposed and even in military intervention by NATO or nation states. The infringement of economic and social rights by a state, however, does not generally trigger a similar response. National sovereignty is more easily invoked by governments when injustice assumes this no less egregious but more problematic form. It seems clear that 'positive' socio-economic rights, although they often appear in human rights declarations and bills of rights, count for less than 'negative' political rights. This discrepancy is normally defended on the ground that even if socio-economic rights were able to be subject to trial in the courts, judges, usually unelected, should not have the power to decide how such economic resources should be distributed. This, it is often contended, is a matter for the legislature rather than the judiciary.

Unhappily, the concept of human rights has been impaired by overuse. Professor James Griffin is justifiably critical in his book, *On Human Rights*, where he writes:

> The term 'human right' is nearly criterionless. There are unusually few criteria for determining when the term is used correctly and when incorrectly – not just among politicians but among philosophers, political theorists and jurisprudents as well. The language of human rights has, in this way, become debased.

Overuse not only diminishes the utility of, but risks disdain for, or even ridicule of, this cherished ideal. The assertion that X or Y is a human right does not make it one. To be fair, there is probably an unavoidable vagueness in the formulation and interpretation of human rights, but it has resulted in the dilution of these rights and a weakening of the protection offered by these declarations.

Several other challenges have been mounted against the concept of human rights. I shall mention only three. The first will be familiar. Utilitarian hostility towards the idea of individual rights is, of course, founded in its wish to maximize the welfare of the general population. The rights or interests of individuals may therefore be forfeited in the name of utility. Liberty is fine but only if it maximizes the general welfare of society. Rights are branded selfish, egotistical and individualist. They function formally but rarely help those who need them most, such as the poor or oppressed.

A second group of detractors, known as relativists, questions whether human rights are really universal. They argue that to say they are is to overlook or neglect local culture, social and political circumstances. Every society is different; societies should therefore shrink from imposing their values on other cultures or religious systems. There are, it is suggested, no absolute moral values that apply to all societies. This is not an easy position to defend. Does morality really depend on local conditions? Those (like Plato – and me) who prefer a 'universalist' view of moral rightness and wrongness reject this form of ethical relativism. Murder is in principle wrong, wherever it happens to be committed. If you hold such a view, you may be accused of being ethnocentric for failing to appreciate social practices from the standpoint of the culture in which they occur. Third, those who embrace a communitarian explanation of justice also target the individualism of human rights which, they claim, neglects community interests, civic virtue and social solidarity. This view is discussed in Chapter 8.

These and other assaults on human rights do not seem to have decreased their popularity. Moreover, despite these misgivings, the concept of human rights has an extremely important function that is sometimes overlooked. Think how oppressors tend to dehumanize their victims. The Jews were dehumanized by the Nazis so as to justify their extermination. The blacks in South Africa were treated as less than human by the South African apartheid government in order to subjugate them. Vesting certain fundamental, inherent, inalienable rights in human beings solely because of their humanity is an effective block against conceiving of some individuals or groups as beyond the pale in order to justify their unjust treatment, or even murder.

Questioning Kant

As already suggested, Kant's unyielding deontological prohibition of lying, torture and suicide rules out cases where circumstances provide strong moral exceptions to this extreme position. Kant's priority of the right over the good means that even if doing the right thing produces a bad result, I am morally bound to do it anyway. This seems counter-intuitive. Suppose Kant is wrong about reason supplying the foundation of morality. What about our emotions, sentiments, passions? If the source of our ethical standards is to be found in our heart rather than our head, does this not wholly extinguish Kant's theory?

This is the view of the Scottish utilitarian, David Hume (1711–1776) who sought to show that our moral duties are not derived from statements of fact. Morality, he argued, is not grounded in our rational judgements but in our emotions. But even if Kant is correct that reason is indeed the basis of morality, we still need to *act* on our moral convictions. Can reason really motivate us to carry out a particular action? Do we not also need to *want* to act? If so, Hume argues, we require the inclination or desire to do the right thing. We may know rationally that it is the right thing but we still need to do it! 'Reason', Hume says, 'is and ought only to be the slave of the passions and can never pretend to any other office than to serve and obey them'. What about our weakness of will? Suppose that I am a good Kantian; my reason tells me to help my friend who is in distress but I ignore his predicament as I am irresistibly drawn to attending a party. The operation of reason has failed to produce the right action.

These expressions of the categorical imperative will not always guarantee a just or fair moral outcome. Apart from omitting our emotions and other motives for acting, its application may often lead to anomalous outcomes. We have already considered some of these; they often take the form of a scenario such as a frightened woman begging you to hide her in your home, as she is being pursued by a killer. You conceal her in your bathroom. A few minutes later an angry man wielding a knife knocks on your door, demanding to know where the woman is. The categorical imperative prohibits you from lying, because that would be to treat the would-be murderer as a means to an end. Or suppose that a terrorist takes a child hostage and uses her as a human shield while threatening to detonate a bomb that would kill thousands of innocent people. The only way to thwart him is to shoot the child; Kant would proscribe using her as a means to an end.

Summing up

Kant's theory of justice, while it strongly champions respect for people as rational, free agents, is generally regarded as too strict to be adopted in the real world. One obvious response is to reject his *duty-based* approach and look to one whose concern is to measure what would produce the best *consequences* for the majority. This is the position adopted by those who adopt a utilitarian approach, as will now become clear.

4 Utilitarianism

Surely, justice simply consists of achieving the greatest happiness for the greatest number? If the majority is happy, will a society not be a just one? This idea is most closely associated with the utilitarian philosophy of Jeremy Bentham (1748–1832), an indefatigable author, campaigner and law reformer. Not until the late 1960s did the extent of his extraordinary productivity become known; many of his manuscripts gathered dust in the University of London for more than a century after his death. His 'extraordinary combination of a fly's eye for detail, with an eagle's eye for illuminating generalizations' led him to condemn many contemporary shibboleths and to produce a wide-ranging theory of, amongst other things, politics, the law, logic and psychology based on the principle of utility.

On his death in 1832, Bentham left instructions for his body to be dissected and then permanently preserved as an 'auto-icon'. For many years, it was publicly displayed in a wooden cabinet in University College, London. On the college's 100th and 150th anniversaries, and in 2013, it 'attended' meetings of the College Council and was recorded in the minutes as 'present but not voting'.

Bentham investigated the operation of the courts, prisons, legal procedure and the reform of numerous branches of the law. His unrelenting, frequently angry, assault on the received wisdom of his day is splendid in its devastating clout, for, as John Stuart Mill put it, Bentham found the battering ram more useful than the builder's trowel. But his most enduring contribution is his utilitarianism which, in some respects, represents an attack on a great deal of eighteenth-century political philosophy. Indeed, Bentham expends a good deal of energy venting his spleen against natural rights (those rights that are not dependent on the law or government but are regarded as *universal and inalienable*), which he dubbed 'nonsense on stilts'. But his method offers considerably more; it has a profound moral foundation. Its premise is that the fundamental objective of morality and justice is that happiness should be maximized. His form of utilitarianism is what the philosopher J.J.C. Smart (1920–2012) calls 'hedonistic'. Bentham's general view is well captured in this important passage from *An Introduction to the Principles of Morals and Legislation*:

> Nature has placed mankind under the governance of two sovereign masters, *pain* and *pleasure*. It is for them alone to point out what we ought to do, as well as to determine what we shall do. On the one hand the standard of right and wrong, on the other the chain of causes and effects, are fastened to their throne … The *principle of utility* recognises this subjection and assumes it for the foundation of that system, the object of which is to rear the fabric of felicity by the hands of reason and of law. Systems which attempt to question it, deal in sounds instead of sense, in caprice instead of reason, in darkness instead of light.

Bentham advances what he calls a 'felicific calculus', a sort of check-list by which to calculate the happiness factor of any act. He identifies twelve pains and fourteen pleasures. In the case of an individual, the significance of a pain or a pleasure is relative to its 'intensity', 'duration', 'certainty or uncertainty' and 'propinquity or remoteness'. Where the purpose is to measure the value of a pleasure or pain in regard to the tendency of an act, two extra conditions must be allowed for: 'fecundity' or 'the chance it has of being followed by sensations of the *same* kind' and 'purity' or 'the chance it has of *not* being followed by sensations of the *opposite* kind'. When we seek to measure the situation of several people, another circumstance is to be considered: the 'extent' or number of people who are affected by the pleasure or pain.

According to Bentham the utility of an act is independent of its motive. Normally, when we do something, our motive is an important factor. But Bentham denies that there can be a 'good' or 'bad' motive; the utility of an act – its goodness or badness – is determined merely by its consequences: the benefits and/or the costs that it causes. Such an emphasis on *consequences* looks to the *future* in its concern to maximize happiness or welfare or some other 'good'. But we need to distinguish between two forms of utilitarianism: 'act utilitarianism' and 'rule utilitarianism'. The former takes the view that the rightness or wrongness of an act is judged by the consequences, good or bad, of the *act itself.* For the latter, rightness or wrongness depends on the goodness or badness of *the consequences of a rule that everyone should perform the action in like circumstances.*

The majority of accounts of utilitarianism (including the one you are now reading) concentrate on *act* utilitarianism, although among legal philosophers it is not uncommon to find appeals made to 'ideal rule utilitarianism', which states that the rightness or wrongness of an action is to be judged by the goodness or badness of a rule that, *if observed*, would have better consequences than any other rule governing the same action. This is applicable, for example, when a judge has to decide whether a plaintiff deserves damages against a defendant: he should disregard the effect of his judgement on the financial circumstances of a *particular* defendant. This form of utilitarianism may, in turn, be differentiated from what is called 'actual rule utilitarianism', which holds that the rightness of an action is to be judged by reference to a rule that is *actually observed* and whose acceptance would maximize utility.

But what are 'consequences'?

Suppose you are stranded on a desert island with no one but a dying man who, in his final hours, entrusts you with $10,000, which he asks you to give to his daughter, Linda, if you ever manage to return to the United States. You promise to do so. After your rescue, you find Linda living in a palatial mansion; she has married a multi-millionaire. The $10,000 will make little difference to her financial situation. Should you not instead donate the money to a struggling charity?

You already know what Kant would say. He is most likely to claim that you should give the money to Linda because you have *promised* to do so. Your action should not be guided by some indefinite *future* result but by an unambiguous *past* fact: your promise. You may well respond that you *do* consider the past fact of your promise, but only in so far as it affects the *total consequences* of your action of giving the money to the charity instead of to Linda. You might also say that it is absurd to argue that you are obliged to keep *every* promise you make. And what about promises you are unable to honour because of some intervening event beyond your control? Suppose you undertake a rigorous search for Linda but are unable to track her down? Surely it is *implied* that the promise is subject to certain indeterminate exceptions.

Contemporary utilitarians prefer the notion of maximizing the extent to which people can attain what they *want*; the emphasis should therefore be on satisfying people's *preferences*. In this way, they are not imposing a conception of 'the good' without incorporating individual choice: you may favour the Beatles over Beethoven or baseball over Bach. It is a matter of subjective choice. This approach has problems of its own, as we shall see. But first we need to look a little closer at Mill's version of utilitarianism.

UTILITARIAN DILEMMAS

The runaway trolley: a trolley is racing down its track, heading straight towards five people who are tied to the track, unable to move. You are standing a little way away, next to a lever. If you pull the lever, the trolley will be switched to a side track. But you notice that there is a person standing on the side track. You have two options: (1) do nothing and allow the trolley to kill the five people on the main track. (2) pull the lever to divert the trolley on to the side track, where it will kill only one person. What should you do?

The fat man: again, the trolley is careering down the track towards the five tied-up people. You are standing on a bridge, beneath which the trolley will pass. You can stop the trolley by placing a very heavy object in front of it. Fortuitously, a very fat man is right next to you. The only way to stop the trolley is to push him over the bridge and on to the track, killing him. This will save the lives of the five people. What should you do?

Jim in the jungle: Jim is a botanist, exploring a wilderness area in South America. He comes across a small town where a local warlord, Pedro, has captured twenty natives, whom he intends to kill. He offers Jim the opportunity to kill one of the natives, in which case he will let the other nineteen go free. What should Jim do?

The organ transplant: A brilliant transplant surgeon has five patients, all certain to die without a transplant. Each needs a different organ. Unfortunately, there are no organs available for any of the five patients. A healthy young traveller, passing through the city in which the surgeon works, arrives for a routine check-up. In the course of it, the doctor discovers that her organs are compatible with all five of his dying patients. If the young woman were to disappear, no one would suspect the doctor. Should the surgeon kill the traveller and give her healthy organs to those five dying people and save their lives?

John Stuart Mill: what do we want?

The son of James Mill, a friend and follower of Jeremy Bentham, John Stuart Mill (1806–1873) began to learn Greek at the age of three and Latin at eight. By the time he reached fourteen, he was well versed in the Greek and Latin classics, had studied history, logic and mathematics, and mastered the fundamentals of economic theory. In his late teens he devoted himself to editing Bentham's manuscripts. Following what he later called his 'mental crisis' of 1826, during which he suffered a nervous breakdown and depression, he reconsidered his earlier ideas and set out on an intellectual journey that would see him become one of the most influential English-speaking philosophers of the nineteenth century. Following Bentham's death in 1832 and his father's four years later, Mill developed his philosophical ideas in books that included *A System of Logic* (1843), *On Liberty* (1859), his celebrated landmark work championing moral and economic freedom, and *Utilitarianism* (1863). He was also an early supporter of women's and animal rights, matters we shall consider in Chapter 10.

Mill recognizes the centrality of Bentham's 'greatest happiness' doctrine. In *Utilitarianism*, he says:

> [A]ctions are right in proportion as they tend to promote happiness, wrong as they tend to produce the reverse of happiness. By happiness is intended pleasure and the absence of pain; by unhappiness, pain and the privation of pleasure.

But Mill rejects the notion that you can *quantify* different pleasures and claims that certain forms of pleasure differ from one another *qualitatively*. Certain higher (largely intellectual) pleasures are worthier, even though they may be less intense than lower (chiefly bodily) pleasures: 'Of two pleasures, if there be one to which all or almost all who have experience of both give a decided preference, irrespective of any feeling of moral obligation to prefer it, that is the more desirable pleasure'. But is this true? Would you prefer reading this book to watching your favourite television show? Don't answer!

Mill insists that we can recognize and value the difference between, say, Mozart and Madonna. 'It is better', he claims, 'to be a human being dissatisfied than a pig satisfied; better to be [the ancient Greek philosopher] Socrates dissatisfied than a fool satisfied'. Nevertheless, he concedes that the achievement of happiness is frequently problematic; hence we may often be morally justified in seeking instead to decrease the amount of pain we experience. Pain, or even forfeiting pleasure, is warranted only when it results directly in the greater good. He does, however, modify the application of utilitarian calculation. In response to the argument that the theory imposes the endless appraisal of the consequences of their conduct on individuals, he permits us generally to be directed by *morality*. In other words, our secondary moral principles provide sufficient guidance for normal daily moral experiences. But nonetheless, he underlines that the value of each specific act, particularly in demanding or controversial cases, is to be determined by reference to the principle of utility.

Mill asks what *motivates* us to do the right thing. Unlike Bentham, he does not confine himself to the *external* sanctions of punishment. He argues that we are also driven by *internal* sanctions such as self-esteem, conscience and guilt. Since we tend to care about others, altruism often suffices to move us to act morally. Even in the absence of others' blame or castigation, I will probably blame myself, and discomfort is among the resultant pains that I reasonably contemplate when determining what to do. Since typically we all desire happiness, argues Mill, it follows that we wish the happiness of everyone. Moreover, the application of utilitarian principles is wholly consistent with our demands for the attainment of *justice*. Justice entails respect for the property, rights and deserts of individuals, as well as basic assumptions of good faith and neutrality. These virtues are effectively sustained by the conscientious application of the principle of utility, Mill claims, because specific cases of each plainly produce the greatest happiness of all parties. Nor, he contends, is it necessary to rely on retributive punishment to support the traditional concept of justice. Mill maintains that the suitably restricted application of external sanctions on utilitarian grounds better accords with appropriate respect for the general welfare.

In *On Liberty* Mill powerfully defends the standpoint that individual freedom is actually based on utilitarian principles:

> It is proper to state that I forego any advantage which could be derived to my argument from the idea of abstract right, as a thing independent of utility. *I regard utility as the ultimate appeal on all ethical questions*; but it must be utility in the largest sense, grounded on the permanent interests of man as a progressive being. Those interests, I contend, authorize the subjection of individual spontaneity to external control, only in respect to those actions of each, which concern the interest of other people.

Mill strongly defends personal (or individual) freedom on the grounds that it increases general happiness. Thus he champions freedom of speech and the right to dissent. He argues that the 'truth' can only be discovered by the unrestricted circulation of ideas. Taken to its logical conclusion, this approach would prevent any inroads being made into the exercise of the right to speak (at least truthfully).

But is Mill's assumption that some objective truth exists 'out there' – and his confidence in the dominance of reason – necessarily correct? It asserts that freedom of expression is a social good because it is the best process by which to advance knowledge and discover truth, starting from the premise that the soundest and most rational judgement is arrived at by considering all the facts and arguments for and against. Yet he goes even further; the minority's view may turn out to be true and so offset the majority's view. In any event, the operation of the free marketplace of ideas should preclude the prevailing opinion hardening into prejudice.

Might this utilitarian mélange of ideas create a society in which the wrong suffered by an individual is overlooked in the interests of the happiness or well-being of the majority? Mill says no. It is wrong, he argues, to compel someone to live according to convention or mainstream belief, because it frustrates that person's achievement of the supreme end of human existence: the full and free enhancement of human faculties. Conformity kills freedom and choice: 'He who does anything because it is the custom, makes no choice … He who lets the world … choose his plan of life for him, has no need of any other faculty than the ape-like one of imitation'. But is Mill abandoning his utilitarian banner here? Is he not appealing to our deepest human nature rather than the common good?

The futility of utility?

Can it work? Is consequentialism in general, and utilitarianism in particular, viable? Is it too crude, too simplistic? Karl Marx dubbed Bentham an 'arch-philistine'; the Scottish writer, Thomas Carlyle (1795–1881) described his theory as 'pig-philosophy'. Central to most of the criticism of utilitarianism is the view that utility neglects the 'separateness of persons'. Its detractors assert that Bentham's deceptively benign maxim 'everybody to count for one and nobody for more than one' actually reduces human beings to *means rather than ends in themselves*. Each person is little more than a number in the calculation of whether general pleasure exceeds general pain. In the words of the jurist H.L.A. Hart (1907–1992), separate individuals are important to utilitarians only in so far as they are 'the channels or locations where what is of value is to be found'. Utilitarianism therefore treats individual people equally but only by effectively treating them as having *no* worth, for their value is not *as persons* but as 'experiencers' of pleasure or happiness.

But perhaps this is not an inevitable feature of utilitarianism. It is at least arguable that *commensurable* values (those that can be compared and traded off against one another) are also *fungible* values (those that are replaceable). Faced with a choice between helping two individuals in distress, a utilitarian is not necessarily insensitive to the plight of the person he cannot assist. He may regard his quandary as a trade-off between the fates of the two people. It could therefore be argued that rather than disregarding the distinctiveness of people, the principle of utility conceives of the problem in terms of a contest between trade-offs, where on the one hand the cost is *negated* by the gain, and on the other where the cost remains lamentable but is merely *outweighed* by the gain.

Whatever the claims of utility, is it really possible to predict and calculate the consequences of one's actions? Can we know what results will follow from what we propose to do? Is there always time to make this assessment? And how far into the future do – or can – we extend the consequences of our actions? In the words of the philosopher Sir Bernard Williams (1929–2003): 'No one can hold that everything, of whatever category, that has value, has it in virtue of its consequences. If that were so, one would just go on for ever and there would be an obviously hopeless regress'. Bentham, however, acknowledges that it is usually impracticable for us to undertake such a calculation before every act. He refers to past experience of the tendency of actions to increase happiness as an adequate guide in most circumstances. We cannot, of course, predict the future with certainty. The best we can do is, from the available alternatives, carry out the action we have most reason to believe will cause the best results.

How persuasive – or realistic – is Bentham's claim that the utility of an act is independent of its motive? Normally when we do something, our motive is an important factor. But Bentham denies that there can be a 'good' or 'bad' motive; the utility of an act – its goodness or badness – is determined merely by its consequences: the benefits and/or the costs that it causes. But surely our motives *are* relevant? Suppose you and I see a baby drowning in a swimming pool. I desperately want to rescue the infant. I dive in but I cannot swim and so fail to save the child. You are an excellent swimmer but choose to walk past, as you have just been to the hairdresser and don't want your hair spoiled. In both cases the consequence is identical – the baby drowns – but our motives are very different. Bentham and Mill claim that each person's act is of equal worth. But can this be right? Are selflessness, love, integrity and other virtues unimportant?

Mill defends his position by arguing that motive is independent of the morality of an *action* but it does have a great deal to do with the worth of the *agent*. Doing the right thing, utilitarians say, is not conclusive evidence of my virtue; a good deed does not necessarily testify to a virtuous character. And bad deeds may spring from virtue. Bentham gives the example of the motive of self-preservation. The desire for self-preservation may result in me killing the sole witness to a crime I have committed; that would be a bad consequence. But if self-preservation encourages me to become a war hero in defence of my country, it would be a good result. My motive does not affect my act but my moral worth.

Is it true, as Bentham asserts, that our pleasure in reading poetry is equal to that of playing pushpin (a children's game in which two pins are placed on the brim of a hat and the participants tap the brim to move the pins to lie across each other)? Are all pleasures really equal? Even Mill's claim that pleasures differ in quality raises the question of how to measure these pleasures. Are we comparing like with like?

Bentham's concept facilitates a simple calculation of pleasure as the exclusive test of morality and it enables a distinction to be drawn between various pleasures in relation to their *quantity*, without admitting to their differences in *quality*. Reading Keats generates more pleasure in terms of what Bentham calls its *fecundity* (or fruitfulness): we are likely to remember the pleasure of reading *Ode to a Nightingale* long after we have read it. Mill claims that given the right education and opportunities, we are able to recognize the distinction between 'higher' and 'lower' pleasures. Our human reason empowers us to differentiate between Haydn and hip-hop and to appreciate the higher pleasures. Why should we regard as valuable only the sum total of pleasure or happiness, abstracted from questions of *distribution* of happiness, welfare and so on? Even if the sum total of units of happiness in a certain society is the same, it could be unfairly distributed. It is possible to rescue utilitarianism from this attack by incorporating a principle of distributive justice (for example merit or equality) into the principle of utility. In a slave society, it is arguable, as J.S. Mill claims, that such a community would not in actual practice yield more utility than one in which goods are fairly distributed.

But should we seek to satisfy people's desires when some desires are unworthy or even contemptible? Think of the sadist torturer or the paedophile. Perhaps this can be explained by the sad reality of the human condition. Bentham lists 'malevolence' amongst both pleasures and pains. The pains of malevolence are those that result from 'the view of any pleasures supposed to be enjoyed by any beings who happen to be the objects of a man's displeasure'. They may also be described as 'the pains of ill-will, of antipathy or the pains of the malevolent or dissocial affections'. There are, he recognizes, twisted people who derive pleasure from inflicting pain on people or animals.

While Kant defines what is good in terms of what is right, it is often argued that utilitarianism defines what is right in terms of what is good. This is tantamount to saying that utilitarianism starts with a notion of what is good (e.g. happiness) and then decides that an action is *right* in so far as it maximizes that good. Some dismiss utilitarianism on the ground that it is concerned only with maximizing welfare; many regard the more important question as the just *distribution* of welfare.

Then there is the question of whether our desires are manipulated by persuasion or advertising. If this is the case, can we separate our 'real' preferences from our 'conditioned' ones? Should utilitarians recommend that people *should* prefer reading Conrad to comic books? If so, how do we justify such a recommendation? If we reply that the principle of utility requires us to, we are saying that the 'felicific calculus' includes not only what we *want* but also what we may one day *decide* to want as a result of persuasion!

Finally, is it really possible, let alone desirable, to weigh my pleasure against your pain? What about decision-makers, such as legislators or judges? When they have to choose between two or more courses of action, can they realistically balance the majority's happiness against a minority's misery?

Summing up

Conceiving of justice as a commodity that can be measured by securing the greatest happiness for the greatest number appears to be a fair, democratic idea. And counting everyone's preferences as having the same value appeals to our sense of equity and equality. But utilitarianism fails to consider people as *individuals* with their own particular needs, rights, duties and desires. It fails, in other words, to treat them with respect. Can justice be reduced to a simple cost-benefit calculation? It cannot, according to John Rawls, whose theory of justice we will now consider.

5
Justice as fairness

Forget about utilitarianism, justice is fundamentally about *fairness*. This argument is at the heart of the most celebrated and influential theory of justice, the work of John Rawls (1921–2002). His account is founded on the ancient idea that the creation of society is based on a social contract among its members.

What exactly is a 'social contract'? One of the earliest incarnations occurs in the Platonic dialogue, *Crito*, where Socrates maintains that he is bound to stay in prison and face the death penalty as a result of his obligation to obey the law, because it has facilitated his way of life and even the very fact of his existence. Remaining in Athens implies a voluntary agreement to abide by its laws. He accepts that, given the justice of the agreement, he is bound by its terms. Socrates therefore acknowledges that our moral and political duties spring from this social contract. Building on earlier social contractarians, in his trail-blazing book, *A Theory of Justice*, Rawls provides what has been described by one of his strongest detractors, the philosopher Robert Nozick, as a 'powerful, deep, subtle, wide-ranging, systematic work … which has not seen its like since the writings of John Stuart Mill, if then. It is a fountain of illuminating ideas, integrated together into a lovely whole'. First, we will briefly consider more modern sources of the social contract.

Hobbes and horror

Thomas Hobbes (1588–1679) lived through the political breakdown that led to the English Civil War; from this experience he developed rational ideas that could form the basis of a state that is resilient to annihilation from within. He believed that even the most repressive government was preferable to the horrifying catastrophe of civil war. To avoid such upheaval, people should be willing to accept absolute political authority, and, to maintain peace and harmony, they should resist any form of rebellion.

Hobbes's argument is founded on the claim he made in his celebrated work, *Leviathan*, that before the social contract the condition of man in his 'natural state' was 'solitary, poor, nasty, brutish and short'. We are naturally disposed toward self-preservation: law and government are therefore required to safeguard order and security. To create an orderly society, we need a social contract under which we relinquish our natural freedom. This is a fairly authoritarian philosophy, which places order above justice. In particular, Hobbes's self-proclaimed purpose is to challenge the legitimacy of revolutions against even wicked governments. His principal concern is to preserve effective government regardless of its form, which always reminds me of the lines from Alexander Pope in his satirical poem *Essay on Man*:

> For forms of government let fools contest;
> Whate'er is best administer'd is best

Hobbes opposes the separation of legislative, judicial and executive powers on the grounds that the loss of one might frustrate the exercise of the others and paralyze government. Restraints on state power would also, he argues, encourage intractable dispute over whether governmental power has been exceeded. Absolute authority is the surest guarantee of stability. He claims that every act we perform, even if apparently altruistic, is really self-serving.

When I give a few coins to a street-sleeper, he suggests what I am actually doing is relishing my power. Any account of human action, including morality must, he says, admit our fundamental egotism. He recognizes our basic mental and physical equality: even the feeblest has the power to slay the strongest. But this equality creates disagreement and discord. We squabble for three key reasons: distrust, competition (for limited supplies of material possessions) and glory (we remain hostile to preserve our powerful reputations). As a result, he concludes, we are in a natural state of perpetual war of all against all, where no morality exists and all live in constant fear. Everyone has a right to everything, including another person's life.

To end this horror of the state of nature, peace is the first law of nature. The second law is that we jointly strip ourselves of certain rights (such as the right to take another person's life) so as to realize peace. This mutual transfer of rights is a *contract* and is the foundation of moral duty. From self-interest, we reciprocally give up rights in order to end the state of war between us. These agreements, Hobbes argues, are not usually effective, since they are based on fear: I live in fear that you will breach your side of the bargain, so no real contract subsists. By our mutual covenant to obey a common authority, we establish 'sovereignty by institution'. Political legitimacy depends not on how a government achieves power but on its ability to protect those who have consented to obey it.

Hobbes is under no illusion that merely concluding agreements can secure peace, so his third law of nature is that such agreements need to be honoured. You know that from self-interest, I may break my contract if I believe I can escape detection. The only sure means of avoiding such a breach, says Hobbes, is to cede unrestricted power to a political sovereign who can punish us if we fail to honour our mutual obligations. Self-interest also explains our willingness to establish an authority with the power to punish. But, according to Hobbes, it is only when such a sovereign exists that we can objectively decide between right and wrong. Hobbes adds a number of other laws, including the fourth: to demonstrate gratitude toward those who comply with contracts. Morality consists wholly of these laws of nature, which are concluded through the social contract.

Locke and liberty

Despite being influenced by Hobbes, John Locke (1632–1704) contests his cynical view of human nature. The social contract, in Locke's view, preserved the natural rights to life, liberty and property and the enjoyment of private rights: the pursuit of happiness engendered, in civil society, the common good. Life before the social contract was not the nightmare described by Hobbes, it was practically paradise!

In his *Two Treatises on Government*, Locke maintains that the state of nature is better than subjugation to the arbitrary power of an absolute sovereign. Nevertheless, this state had a serious defect: property was inadequately protected. To resolve this, man relinquished, under a social contract, some of his liberty. Locke bases his philosophy on an interpretation of man's rights and responsibilities under God. It is a complex, intricate attempt to elucidate the operation of the social contract and its terms in which two central ideas stand out. First, when a government is unjust or authoritarian, Locke recognizes the right of 'oppressed people' to 'resist tyranny' and to rebel against the government: 'a tyrant has no authority'. Second, one of the more influential features of his theory is the emphasis he places on the right to *property*: God owns the earth and has given it to us to enjoy; there can therefore be no right of property. But by mixing his labour with material objects, the labourer acquires the right to the thing he has created. In the state of nature, everything is commonly owned but as God gave man reason and senses to employ for his preservation and reproduction, whatever he takes from the state of nature with his own hands he converts into his own property. This is both natural and just.

Unlike Hobbes, whose priority was to keep a government – any government – in place, Locke preferred a *limited* form of government: the checks and balances among branches of government and the genuine representation in the legislature would, in his view, curtail government and maximize individual liberties. His arguments in support of the social contract and the right of citizens to rebel against their king were extremely influential on the democratic revolutions in the United States, especially on Thomas Jefferson and the drafting of the Declaration of Independence and the constitution. The importance Locke attached to the protection of property has seen him both celebrated as the source of the idea of private ownership and vilified as the precursor of modern capitalism. In the next chapter, we shall observe the impact of his ideas on one prominent modern philosopher.

Rousseau's 'general will'

The concept of a social contract in the writing of Jean-Jacques Rousseau (1712–1778) stimulated the ideological fervour that led to the French Revolution. His book *The Social Contract* begins with the oft-quoted line: 'Man was born free and he is everywhere in chains'. Humans were free in the state of nature but progress has undermined that freedom, as it generates subservience to, and reliance on, others as well as social and economic inequalities. We cannot return to the state of nature, so the objective of politics is to reinstate our freedom, reuniting who we really are with how we live together.

This is the essential challenge that *The Social Contract* pursues: how can we be both free and live harmoniously together without the pressure exercised by others? We can do so, Rousseau believes, by submitting our individual, particular wills to the collective or 'general will', which is fashioned through agreement with other free and equal people. Since we are born free and equal, nobody has a natural right to govern others and consequently the only justified authority is that which springs from agreement.

For Rousseau, the social contract represents an agreement between the individual and the community by which the individual becomes part of the 'general will'. The community governs what is good for society as a whole. The social contract is expressed as: 'Each of us puts his person and all his power in common under the supreme direction of the general will; and in a body we receive each member as an indivisible part of the whole'.

Rousseau's notion of the general will is combined with his concept of sovereignty that, in his view, is not merely legitimate political power but its exercise in pursuit of the public good and therefore of the general will. Its purpose is 'general' in the sense that it can institute rules, social classes or even a monarchy, but it can never stipulate who exactly the *individuals* are who are subject to the rules, members of the classes or the rulers. To specify the identity of these individuals would, he says, weaken the fundamental idea that the general will advances the good of the *society as a whole* rather than an association of individual wills that place their *own* desires, or those of particular groups, above the needs of the community as a whole. Indeed, he differentiates the general will from an assembly of individual wills. In Book 2 of *The Social Contract* he writes:

> There is often a great deal of difference between the will of all and the general will. The latter looks only to the common interest; the former considers private interest and is only a sum of private wills. But take away from these same wills the pluses and minuses that cancel each

other out and the remaining sum of the differences is the general will.

He imagines three different kinds of will. First, individuals all have *private wills* matching their selfish interests. Second, individuals, in their backing for the collective and their role as citizens, selflessly treat the general will of that *collective* as their own and support laws that enable co-existence under conditions of equal freedom. And third, individuals may identify with the shared will of a *group* within the community.

In a well-organized society, no tension arises between private and general will, because people recognize that justice and their self-interest necessitate that they acquiesce to a law that defends their freedom by protecting them from the violence and control of others. Rousseau concedes that few societies achieve this degree of discipline and harmony. Some individuals will inevitably resist constraints on their freedom dictated by the general will. Others may coalesce into rival factions and one bloc may inflict its will on the state.

Accordingly, Rousseau's infamous proposition that man must 'be forced to be free' is generally interpreted to mean that individuals surrender their free will to create popular sovereignty. The law, says Rousseau, may legitimately encroach on individuals' natural rights. In fact, as long as government represents the general will it may do practically anything. Hence, although championing democracy, he is prepared to invest the legislature with almost unlimited power by virtue of it representing the general will. Rousseau is therefore a paradox: a democrat and a totalitarian. Nevertheless, as the general will intercedes only when it would be in the interests of society as a whole, Rousseau's ostensible authoritarianism is alleviated by the prominence he accords liberty and equality. We could construe an intervention by the sovereign as necessary only to enhance liberty and equality, not to weaken them. This balance between the absolute power of the state and the rights of individuals is founded on a social contract that shields society against factional, sectional and class interests.

A portrait of Rousseau was the only painting hung on the walls of Immanuel Kant's home, and it is said that the only occasion when Kant forgot to take his daily walk was when he was immersed in Rousseau's treatise on education, *Emile*! There is evidence of Rousseau's powerful influence on Kant in, for example, the third formulation of the categorical imperative (the 'formula of the kingdom of ends'), which echoes the account of the general will in *The Social Contract*.

John Rawls and the social contract

Having sketched the philosophies of his illustrious forebears, especially Bentham, Mill, Kant, Hobbes, Locke and Rousseau, we are now in a position, I hope, to consider the leading effort to formulate a comprehensive theory of justice for our time. The significance of the work of the twentieth-century Harvard philosopher John Rawls cannot be overstated. His book, *A Theory of Justice,* is crammed with ideas that continue to dominate contemporary discussions of justice. Rawls's theory draws largely on a Kantian analysis of people and their capacities. His social contractarian theory of justice preserves a broadly Kantian moral system of universal rights but avoids Kant's more idealistic concepts. He says his theory, which he calls 'justice as fairness', adopts a Kantian view of people as 'free and equal,' morally independent, rational agents, who are not necessarily egoists. He also declares clearly that his theory is a better alternative to utilitarianism: he attempts to keep the moral baby and throw out the metaphysical bathwater.

The social contract

Rawls's theory of justice as fairness springs from the idea of a social contract, although it does not take the same form as its antecedents. His project is well expressed in this important paragraph from *A Theory of Justice*:

> My aim is to present a conception of justice which generalises and carries to a higher level of abstraction the familiar theory of the social contract as found, say, in Locke, Rousseau and Kant. In order to do this we are not to think of the original contract as one to enter a particular society or to set up a particular form of government. Rather, the guiding idea is that the principles of justice for the basic structure of society are the object of *the original agreement*. They are the principles that *free and rational persons* concerned to further *their own interests* would accept in an *initial position of equality* as defining the fundamental terms of their association. These principles are to regulate all further agreements; they specify the kinds of social cooperation that can be entered into and the forms of government that can be established. This way of regarding the principles of justice I shall call *justice as fairness.*

This articulates both the letter and the spirit of Rawls's theory of justice. The phrases that I have italicized are key elements in his social contractarian argument, whose attraction lies in the detachment, or neutrality, it pursues. We should, he maintains, distinguish between people's authentic judgements of justice and their subjective, egoistic opinions. In this way we shall see that the view taken by an imaginary dispassionate outsider concerning what constitutes a just decision is likely to be more reasonable than any position we have as individuals with a vested interest in the consequences of that decision. A similar concern for detached, dispassionate deliberation is manifested by the jury system, which attempts to achieve a just outcome in a trial by employing a process conducted by individuals who have no connection to the case being tried.

The next step is to test these objectively acquired principles against our subjective judgement. The unavoidable discrepancy between the two needs to be adjusted by modifying our judgement so that we arrive at a position in which the two are alike, when we reach what Rawls calls 'reflective equilibrium'. In this state, all our beliefs form a coherent whole. For example, I may believe that torture is always wrong; this supports my more general political opinion in favour of individual rights, which, in turn, affirms my much more abstract conviction that everyone deserves freedom and equality. The pieces fit neatly together like a jigsaw puzzle. Seamless reflective equilibrium is not always achievable but the method may be employed to improve and explain the justification for our moral and political views.

No to utilitarianism

A significant element in Rawls's theory of justice is his rejection of utilitarianism. He regards it as an unacceptable means by which to conceive of, or measure, justice. Social inequality is unacceptable, even if it advances maximum welfare. This opposition is based partly on the Kantian premise of the separateness or distinctness of individual people, which utilitarianism disdains, and partly on his position that justice comes before happiness or, as philosophers like to say, 'the right is prior to the good'.

The original position

Rawls is often misunderstood as suggesting that the people in the original position (the POP) actually exist or existed. He makes it clear at the outset that it should not be thought of as 'an actual historical state of affairs, much less as a primitive condition of culture'. It is to be understood as a 'purely hypothetical situation characterized so as to lead to a certain conception of justice'. It is, in other words, a heuristic, or diagnostic, device to facilitate the construction of a neutral view of the essential elements of a just society. As with previous social contractarians (Hobbes, Locke and Rousseau) the idea is of an *imaginary* gathering of individuals, each shrouded in a 'veil of ignorance', debating the principles of justice. They do not know to which sex, class, religion or social position they belong. They don't know in what time or country they are living, and have only a rudimentary acquaintance with the laws of science and psychology.

Ignorance is often said to be bliss. For the POP it is bliss with a purpose. They must decide unanimously on the general principles that will settle the terms under which they will live as a society. What would you do? On the basis of our rational self-interest, surely most of us would support the principles that give us the greatest chance of attaining our idea of the good life. In *A Theory of Justice*, Rawls claims the POP, stripped of their uniqueness and individuality, will eventually come down in favour of two principles:

> *First principle*: 'Each person is to have an equal right to the most extensive total system of equal basic liberties compatible with a similar system of liberty for all'.
> *Second principle*: 'Social and economic inequalities are to be arranged so that they are both:
>
> (a) to the greatest benefit of the least advantaged, consistent with the just savings principle
> (b) attached to offices and positions open to all under conditions of fair equality of opportunity'

The first principle of equal basic liberties relates to the formulation of the political constitution. The second principle applies mainly to economic institutions. Implementation of the first principle assumes priority over the second principle. Within the second principle, fair equality of opportunity takes priority over the difference principle. *Liberty is placed above equality* because of what Rawls calls the 'maximin' strategy: no one wants to risk his liberty when the veil of ignorance is lifted and it is discovered that they are among the poorest members of society.

RAWLS: CRITICS' COMPLIMENTS

Robert Nozick: 'a powerful, deep, subtle, wide-ranging, systematic work in political and moral philosophy which has not seen its like since the writings of John Stuart Mill, if then. It is a fountain of illuminating ideas, integrated together into a lovely whole. Political philosophers now must either work within Rawls's theory or explain why not.'

Ronald Dworkin: 'No theorist has made a greater contribution to legal philosophy in modern times than the political philosopher, John Rawls ... I offer you a confession but with no apology. Each of us has his or her own Immanuel Kant and from now on we will struggle, each of us, for the benediction of John Rawls. After all the books, all the footnotes, all the wonderful discussions, we are only just beginning to grasp how much we have to learn from that man.'

But how could this work in practice? Take the difference principle. Compare the huge wealth of someone like Mark Zuckerberg, the super-rich founder of Facebook, with the poverty of the least well-off members of American society. Could the application of the difference principle really help the poor? Rawls would not deny Zuckerberg his fortune; he encourages the talented to develop their abilities but, as a matter of justice, he proposes the difference principle which, he says, would operate for the benefit of the poor. For example, by imposing a heavy tax on the likes of

Zuckerberg, the poor could be provided with improved welfare, health care and education and inequalities between rich and poor could be narrowed.

A society governed by his two principles, Rawls argues, is better than a utilitarian society. Securing equal basic liberties for all fosters a spirit of collaboration based on mutual respect; it eliminates clashes about whether certain groups may be denied equal rights. A utilitarian society, on the other hand, could be torn apart by distrust, as various groups argue that average utility could be increased by applying programmes that cause social division and disagreement. The 'maximin' strategy may be explained by Rawls's gain and loss table, which I have adapted in Table 2.

Table 2: Rawls's gain and loss table

	C1	**C2**	**C3**
D1	–£700	£800	£1200
D2	–£800	£700	£1400
D3	£500	£600	£800

D = Decisions C = Circumstances

Which is the best outcome among the three possible decisions? If I select D1 and C1 occurs, I will lose £700 but if C2 occurs I will gain £800 and, if I am really lucky and C3 occurs, I will gain £1200. The same process is applied to decisions D2 and D3. The gain (*g*) depends on my decision, *d,* and the circumstances, *c.* Which decision should I make? The 'maximin' principle directs me to elect D3 because in this event the *worst* that can happen to me is that I gain £500, which is better than the worst for the other actions (in which I could lose either £800 or £700).

Likewise, the POP, as rational individuals, would select principles that ensure that the worst condition they might find themselves in, when the veil of ignorance is raised, is the least undesirable of the available alternatives. The same reasoning applies that would result in the POP choosing the 'maximin' rule, says Rawls. They will go for clause (a) of the second principle, the so-called '*difference principle*', because it ensures that people have certain inviolable rights. This is an essential feature of a liberal society.

The POP will, crucially, be best placed to improve their condition in a society that places liberty above equality, because various 'social primary goods' (which Rawls defines to include rights, liberties, powers, opportunities, income, wealth and, especially, self-respect) are more likely to be achieved in a liberal society. And they would choose the difference principle for another reason: it is better than its two main rivals, the 'system of natural liberty' and the notion of 'fair equality of opportunity'. The former implies an unrestricted market economy with no commitment to redistribute wealth. The POP would reject this principle, he argues, because it 'permits distributive shares to be improperly influenced by … factors so arbitrary from a moral point of view'. This might arise where you happen to be born into a rich family, which from a moral point of view is irrelevant.

The idea of 'fair equality of opportunity' allows individuals' prospects to flourish on the basis of their natural talent and the energies they expend in developing them effectively. This is superior to the system of natural liberty but it is, in Rawls's view, open to a similar objection: why should my talents be any more morally relevant than the fact that I am the son of a billionaire? In neither case are these accidents related to what I deserve (the principle of *desert)*. By selecting the difference principle, my natural talents may increase my wealth only if, in the process, they also increase the wealth of the *least advantaged*.

The second principle includes a significant restriction, to protect the interests of the least advantaged from the social arrangements selected. Rawls calls this the 'just savings principle' which specifies that the POP need to ask themselves how much money they would be willing to save at each stage of advance, on the assumption that all other generations will save at the same rates. Rawls contends that the welfare of future generations is important: what a society saves, and what burdens it thereby imposes, is matters of justice. It is based on the idea that:

> … each generation must not only preserve the gains of culture and civilization and maintain intact those institutions that have been established but it must also put aside in each period of time a suitable amount of real capital accumulation. This saving may take various forms, from net investment in machinery and other means of production to investment in learning and education.

The principle therefore:

> … assigns an appropriate rate of accumulation to each level of advance. Presumably this rate changes depending upon the state of society. When people are poor and saving is difficult, a lower rate of saving should be required; whereas in a wealthier society greater savings may reasonably be expected since the real burden is less. Eventually once just institutions are firmly established, the net accumulation required falls to zero.

This ensures that the POP will decide to save some of their resources for future generations, because they have no idea in what kind of time the citizens they represent live. They do not necessarily have to select a savings principle that entails infinite economic growth. Instead, they may choose zero real growth until a generation arises in which the two principles are fulfilled.

Rawls applies his theory of justice to the question of civil disobedience, which he defines as 'a public, nonviolent, conscientious yet political act contrary to law usually done with the aim of bringing about a change in the law or policies of the government'. In the case of a fundamentally unjust society (such as Nazi Germany or apartheid South Africa) citizens may feel that they are morally obliged to disobey obviously unjust laws that discriminate against members of a particular religion or race. But Rawls states that before they are morally justified in breaking the law, three conditions must be satisfied. First, such action should normally address violations of equal civil liberties (the first principle of justice) and/or of 'fair equality of opportunity' (the second part of the second principle), with violations of the difference principle (the first part of the second principle) being less clear and therefore more difficult to justify. Second, any act of civil disobedience should follow only after appeals to the political majority have been reasonably tried and failed. Third, it must be likely that the disobedience will achieve more good than harm for society. Nevertheless, even if all three of these conditions are met, and the action seems justified, there is still the question of whether, in practice, it would be 'wise or prudent,' to engage in the act of civil disobedience. Examples of civil disobedience that would appear to meet Rawls's conditions include Mahatma Ghandi's peaceful campaign for Indian independence, the civil rights movement in the United States led by Martin Luther King Jr and the struggle against apartheid in South Africa.

Getting down to work

Once they have agreed the two principles and the principle of 'just savings', the veil of ignorance is slightly lifted to enable the POP to *adapt* the general principles to the actual circumstances of the society of the citizens they represent. The POP are now provided with more material about the society's political culture and economic development. They then begin to draft a constitution that reflects the two principles. Their overriding purpose is to establish a system of liberties to enable citizens to develop their abilities and pursue their individual concepts of the good. They must decide on the most appropriate institutions necessary to achieve political equality. This, insists Rawls, must include the public funding of elections, limits on campaign contributions and equal access to the media, otherwise the political process will be hijacked by private economic power.

Rawls stresses that equality of opportunity requires more than simply checking discrimination in education and employment. The state must also support decent education for the less well off and a basic minimum wage and universal health care. But Rawls unequivocally eschews the welfare state on the grounds that welfare state capitalism licenses control of the economy to a group of wealthy private parties. It does not provide adequate resources to have even approximately equal political, employment or educational opportunities and tends to produce a dispirited underclass. But even worse at promoting equality, Rawls argues, is the system of laissez-faire capitalism. Nor can a socialist command economy secure equality since excessive state power imperils political equality and basic liberties such as freedom of choice in the job market.

Rawls claims that his model of justice as fairness favours a form of democratic socialism or a *property-owning democracy* whose government endorses extensive ownership of productive assets and comprehensive access to education and training. Democratic socialism has similar aims but contains worker-managed firms. Both political arrangements seek to empower all citizens, including the least advantaged, to manage their own affairs within a framework of substantial social and economic equality. This is a matter of 'basic justice'.

Fine-tuning

Following the publication of *A Theory of Justice* in 1971, Rawls refined his ideas in a number of essays, concluding in 1993 with the publication of his book, *Political Liberalism*. In this, he attempts to eliminate some of the assumptions present in *A Theory of Justice* and adopts a more communitarian approach, arguing that his idea of the person as impartial citizen offers the best account of liberal-democratic political culture and that his objective is to establish the rules for consensus in political communities where citizens seek it. At its heart is an attempt to consider the relationship between religion and democracy and how widely held moral, religious and philosophical worldviews can co-exist peacefully in a liberal society.

Responding to critics of his earlier book, Rawls seeks to clarify his position and correct misconceptions that his earlier work (itself the outcome of a similar process) produced. In particular, he rejects the idea that his principles of justice were intended to be a sort of Archimedean point in ethics that offered a universal standard of social justice. His intention was to offer a theory that applies to modern constitutional democracies. It is, as the title suggests, a *political* concept of justice, in contrast to a moral, religious or philosophical notion of the good. His theory thus has modest claims: the idea of 'justice as fairness' is a *political* rather than an epistemological or metaphysical task. It is, in other words, a conception of justice that is essentially practical.

Political power is justifiable in a free society when its use conforms to a political concept of justice. But why would citizens agree to observe the laws generated by a particular concept when there may be major differences in their political opinions? Rawls pins his hopes on the existence of an '*overlapping consensus*'. This offers a better prospect for stability than what he calls a mere modus vivendi model. He postulates his two principles of justice as the terms under which members of a pluralist, democratic society, with rival interests and values, could achieve political harmony. His idea of political liberalism recognizes that this consensus may be threatened by the development of a shared moral or religious doctrine. But, he suggests, the community's sense of justice would triumph over the state's particular version of the public good.

Within this overlapping consensus, citizens will back the same laws for different reasons. A political concept is self-supporting: it is a 'module' that can be accommodated into a variety of perspectives held by citizens, who will support this shared 'module' from within their own distinct viewpoints. This provides the best foundation of democratic stability, which is preferable to an inevitably fluctuating balance of power among citizens with diverse outlooks. The attraction of an overlapping consensus is that citizens morally endorse a political concept enthusiastically from within their own perceptions and this support will endure even in the face of the loss of power by their particular group.

Rawls has no illusions about the attainability or durability of an overlapping consensus. Not every society will have sufficient shared common interest to unite in support of a liberal concept of justice. Irrational, repressive policies can also emerge and crush liberal values. But is an overlapping consensus the best hope for stability and justice? Rawls dismisses the idea that this is an unreasonably idealistic, utopian vision. Are you convinced? It may be that the difference principle becomes more difficult to accept under these conditions. And it is questionable whether the principle can be applied without some judgement about what constitutes 'equality'. For example, is 'equal pay' related to necessity, production, exertion or the importance or value of the labour?

In 1999 Rawls further re-evaluated his views in *Law of Peoples*, where he goes so far as to concede that liberalism may not be appropriate to all societies and proffers a model of what he calls a 'decent, well-ordered society' that liberal societies ought to accept, even if it is undemocratic, provided it abstains from aggression against other societies and exhibits a 'common good conception of justice', a 'reasonable consultation hierarchy' and protects basic human rights. His account largely follows the twin ideas of justice as fairness and political liberalism. His purpose is to show how many of the evils of history, such as oppression, genocide, unjust wars, religious persecution and so on, result from political injustice. Once this is eradicated and replaced by just institutions, the iniquity will ultimately wane. Without well-ordered, just, or nearly just, political institutions, the prospects for global justice (to be considered in Chapter 12) are bleak.

Qualms and quibbles

Unsurprisingly, not everyone is happy with Rawls's theory of justice, even in its modified form. While it has won numerous plaudits, his theory has attracted strong criticism from various quarters. The attacks range from a general unease about his whole project (his social contractarianism and his 'deep theory') to specific attacks on details of the conceptual tools he employs (the 'original position', the 'difference principle', 'reflective equilibrium', the 'maximin rule' and so on). To give you a flavour of the kinds of onslaughts that have been made, I will sketch a few here, the most important will be considered in greater detail in later chapters.

Some critics complain that the 'original position', even as a heuristic device, is defective. They allege that it is mistaken to imagine that people can actually be stripped of their values. There are also critics who doubt whether this fundamental concept in Rawls's theory would inevitably produce the outcome that he assumes. Ronald Dworkin (1931–2013) argues that at the core of Rawls's 'deep theory' is the right of each individual to equal concern and respect. But, says Dworkin, this right is a consequence not of the social contract but an assumption of Rawls's application of the contract. The economist and Nobel laureate Amartya Sen dislikes Rawls's focus on just *institutions.* He prefers to look at the 'actual realizations' of justice in particular societies. Instead of a Rawlsian transcendental approach to justice, he proposes a 'reasoned approach' in regard to the nature of a 'just society', in which feasible alternatives are compared and chosen. We will look at his so-called 'capability approach' in Chapter 7.

A similar critique queries whether the POP would *necessarily* opt for Rawls's two principles and, even if they did, whether they would – or should – prefer liberty to equality. What about the risk-taker who might go for a winner-takes-all approach? Others wonder how conflicts between basic liberties are to be resolved. Some have identified a clash between Rawls's first and second principles: don't inequalities in wealth and power inevitably create inequalities in basic liberty? But Rawls does not claim that the principles of justice are fixed; they are provisional ideas that are subject to democratic debate concerning the kind of society we wish to establish.

Some of Rawls's detractors detect a 'bias' in the theory. Not surprisingly, those who adopt a Marxist analysis contend that Rawls makes several traditional, 'bourgeois, liberal assumptions'. It is alleged that he regards people as naturally 'free' but, Marxists argue, individuals are mostly a product of their class interests. Likewise, his concept of the state employs a consensus rather than a conflict model of society. One critic claims that in a class-divided society (in which no institutional arrangement acceptable to the best-off is acceptable to the worst-off) the difference principle is unlikely to be chosen by the representatives of the best-off. Rawls's theory therefore assumes a non-egalitarian structure of society.

Similarly, those who embrace a communitarian view of justice find in Rawls's individualism an inadequate account of what it is to be a person. The starting-point of the communitarian view, presented persuasively and prominently by Michael Sandel, is that individuals are partially defined by their communities. I will discuss this approach in Chapter 11. Many feminist writers are equally unconvinced by Rawls's assumptions. Carole Pateman (1940–) has argued that the device of a social contract conceals a more important contract regarding men's relationship to women. While contract theory is characterized as against patriarchy, in reality it embodies men's control over women. This power, she claims, exists in at least three typical modern contracts: marriage, prostitution and the contract for surrogate motherhood. Each exemplifies male control and shows how the contract is a tool by which men dominate women. Other feminist writers have questioned the very nature of the person at the core of contract theory. The 'liberal individual' is ostensibly classless, 'raceless' and genderless. But is this archetype not loaded in favour of a rather specific sort of person? Is there not, some have pointedly asked, a tendency in social contract theory to define our rights and duties without considering those relationships that determine our moral obligations such as the mother-child bond? To understand human relations in purely contractual terms fails to account for our complete moral experience.

The difference principle (which provides that social and economic inequalities are to the greatest benefit of the least advantaged members of society) has been attacked from various perspectives. Utilitarians dislike the difference principle because it fails to ensure the greatest happiness of the greatest number; in modern language, it does not maximize utility. One critique alleges that it presumes that our natural talents are a 'collective asset'. If they are, Robert Nozick argues, the same could be said for our bodily organs. Some have questioned whether the difference principle genuinely promotes equality or merely makes everyone worse off. Why, it has been asked, should those with talents (who can benefit only when it assists the least well off) agree to do so? Suppose they prefer to work less diligently or simply fail to develop their talents at all? If, to assist the poor, they are required to pay a higher rate of income tax, surely they will, instead of particle physics, choose pen-pushing as a career? Rawls allows an exception to equality in such circumstances; he concedes that it may be necessary to offer incentives to improve the condition of the poor. Where incentives stimulate economic growth so as to put the poor in a better position than they would be under circumstances of equality, the difference principle would countenance them. Rawls's concept of 'social primary goods' has also been attacked: would the POP necessarily choose these things (rights, power, money and so on) in preference to, say, a caring society in which all are treated as equals? Does it not assume that people are acquisitive, greedy and selfish?

More disparaging is the assertion that Rawls fails to offer a theory of justice at all! According to certain critics, justice fundamentally concerns *deserts*: it is fair and just that we should get what we *deserve*. If you work hard, you deserve the rewards. But, in Rawls's formula, hard work need be rewarded only to ensure that the worst-off do as well as possible. He says: 'For a society to organize itself with the aim of rewarding moral desert as a first principle would be like having the institution of property in order to punish thieves'.

No less challenging is the attack mounted by Martha Nussbaum who argues that Rawls neglects three problems of social justice: the problem of fairness for the disabled, to 'all world citizens' and to non-human animals (see Chapter 10). There are also those who, like Robert Nozick (to be discussed in the next chapter), condemn the very concept of a patterned distribution of social goods.

It is hardly surprising that a work of the ambition and depth of *A Theory of Justice* should attract dissatisfaction and disagreement. I don't imagine that, distinguished scholar though he was, John Rawls could have regarded his monumental work to be immune from all attack. Indeed, in his preface he states that three different versions of his manuscript were read and commented on by his colleagues and students, concedes that he has 'not been able to deal with all of their criticisms,' and recognizes that he is 'well aware of the faults that remain'. Rawls set himself a mammoth task; at its heart is his simple claim that justice is the first virtue of social institutions. The book's 600 pages – a book whose English edition has sold half a million copies and been translated into thirty languages – provide a comprehensive, meticulously reasoned alternative to utilitarianism. The last lines of this classic (which in my copy of the first edition, betraying my age, I have both underlined *and* highlighted), conclude his long treatise with these stirring words:

> The perspective of eternity is not a perspective from a certain place beyond the world, nor the point of view of a transcendent being; rather it is a certain form of thought and feeling that rational persons can adopt within the world. And having done so, they can, whatever their generation, bring together into one scheme all individual perspectives and arrive together at regulative principles that can be affirmed by everyone as he lives by them, each from his own standpoint. Purity of heart, if one could attain it, would be to see clearly and to act with grace and self-command from this point of view.

I hope that in this passage you can hear the echoes of Kant, Rousseau and Locke.

Summing up

Disparities in wealth and opportunity are present in every society. The injustice that flows from their unfair distribution is a challenge to any theory of justice. By means of his hypothetical social contract, Rawls postulates two principles of justice that he argues the people in the original position would choose. His difference principle seeks to correct this imbalance, without discouraging gifted individuals from pursuing their goals, however materialistic, but subject to the condition that the fruits of their talents also belong to society at large as a common asset. The notion of wealth-sharing is fundamental to Rawls's theory of justice but this restriction on the liberty of the rich to keep what they earn makes libertarians unhappy, as we shall now discover.

6 Libertarianism

Libertarians champion liberty as the main goal of society. They want to maximize individual freedom and autonomy and stress the importance of political freedom and individual choice. In general they are suspicious of authority and tend to advocate laissez-faire capitalism and private property.

The distribution of wealth in most 'free' societies is determined by the market, which most theories of justice acknowledge as a fact of life. Indeed, even Rawls's difference principle employs the market as a means of helping the least advantaged. Utilitarians use it to achieve a distribution that maximizes utility, and desert-based theories rely on the market to distribute goods according to desert. On the other hand, those who support libertarian distributive principles seldom regard the market as a means to a particular pattern. Their approach rejects the idea of any patterned distribution; rather, it considers market transactions as just in their own right. This means that as long as people acquire or exchange their acquisitions justly, nothing more need be said. No particular patterned distribution is required for a society to be just. The state ought positively to *refrain* from interfering with the property held by its citizens; it should keep its hands off what I have lawfully acquired: I am entitled to it.

This so-called 'entitlement' theory of justice is most effectively advanced by the American political philosopher Robert

Nozick (1938–2002) in his book *Anarchy, State and Utopia.* His attack on distributive justice has generated considerable controversy. One critic even accused Nozick of an indecent desire to starve the poor and abandon the sick, old and disabled. The validity of this, and other, charges should become clear in the course of this chapter.

A 'night watchman' state

Going further than Rawls in rejecting utilitarianism, Nozick argues that respect for individual rights is the fundamental standard by which to assess state action and therefore the only legitimate state is a minimal one that restricts its activities to the protection of the rights of life, liberty, property and contract. Nozick wishes to limit the role of the state to that of a 'night watchman', its job restricted to defence, policing and judicial administration. Everything else (education, health, welfare and so on) ought to be the responsibility of the private sector: charities, churches and other bodies in civil society. The market, he argues, is more efficient than government in carrying out these sorts of tasks. Nozick's reasoning rests on moral, libertarian grounds. He contends that, whatever its practical advantages, a libertarian society's most compelling justification is its respect for individual rights.

Nozick is strongly influenced by the works of the Nobel prize-winning economist and philosopher, F.A. Hayek (1899–1992), principally *The Road to Serfdom* and *The Constitution of Liberty,* which, along with the novels of Ayn Rand (1905–1992) challenge the very idea of wealth distribution as proposed, in particular, by Rawls. Borrowing both from Kant (that people should never be treated as means) and Locke (that we own ourselves) Nozick develops the notion of self-ownership to the point where we have rights over our bodies and our abilities and hence the fruits of our labour and talents. We are, as individuals, ends rather than means; this fact generates certain *rights*, including the Lockean right to the fruits of our work. When we own an object we have the right to destroy it or transfer it to another. Similarly, owning myself confers rights on the various parts that constitute me. Such rights operate as 'side constraints' on your action: you cannot injure or kill me, for this would be tantamount to destroying or damaging my property. Nor can you remove any of my organs to transplant into someone else; that would be theft of my property.

Nozick adopts another aspect of Lockean thought, the view that our moral rights as individuals are 'state of nature rights' that precede legal and political institutions. But they also afford a standard by which we can evaluate and constrain both the actions of individuals and groups and also those of institutions. Harking back to Locke, he contends that these moral rights arise *prior to any social contract*. Even without a social contract, they impose moral constraints on individuals, groups and institutions.

It is fundamental to the Nozickian ideal that every individual has pre-contractual moral rights against certain things being done to them, even for morally or socially desirable ends. Thus, utilitarianism cannot provide a just outcome because 'there is no moral outweighing of one of our lives by others so as to lead to a great overall social good. There is no justified sacrifice of some of us for others'. Nozick goes further than Rawls in this rejection of utility; he claims that to impose a sacrifice on an individual in pursuit of any desirable social benefit is unacceptable because it treats individuals as means rather than ends.

Taxation as slavery

His radical libertarian approach leads Nozick to reject the redistribution of wealth. When the state taxes my income (the fruits of my hard work) it is a form of slavery. The wealth that I have produced is taken from me by duress. The state accrues a right to some of the proceeds of my labour, hence it *owns* part of me, which contradicts the principle of self-ownership:

> Seizing the results of someone's labor is equivalent to seizing hours from him and directing him to carry on various activities ... This process whereby they take this decision from you makes them a *part-owner* of you; it gives them a property right in you. Just as having such partial control and power of decision, by right, over an animal or inanimate object would be to have a property right in it.

The 'nanny state', with its prohibitions and regulations about food, health and safety, censorship, minimum wage and the like is anathema to Nozick. He argues that since the state is 'intrinsically immoral', it may not seek to redistribute resources in pursuit of equality. A state that seeks to distribute wealth in society requires excessive powers and therefore infringes the individual freedom that is based on a Kantian 'separateness of persons'.

Keeping what's yours

It is evident that Nozick is more concerned with protecting individuals' rights to *what they already have, rather than what others may not have*. Nozick's 'entitlement theory' of justice is based on three sets of principles:

- *Principles of acquisition*: to determine the circumstances under which persons are able to acquire ownership of previously unowned resources.
- *Principles of transfer*: to decide the methods by which the ownership of resources may be transferred between persons.
- *Principles of rectification*: to define how an *unjust* acquisition or transfer of property should be rectified (e.g., where property has been acquired fraudulently).

Nozick imagines a society in which wealth is distributed in a way that does *not* respect the entitlement of persons, such as one which favours an equal distribution, although it could equally be one based on desert or enterprise. He calls this distribution D1. An opponent of Nozick's model would accept this as a just distribution, since Nozick has permitted his adversary to select it. Suppose, he says, that among the members of this society is the outstanding basketball player, Wilt Chamberlain, who has a condition in his contract with his team that he will play only if every spectator places twenty-five cents into a special box at the entrance of the stadium. The contents of the box will be given to him. Suppose that over the course of the season, a million fans part with twenty-five cents each to see him play. The result will be a new distribution, D2, in which Chamberlain is richer by $250,000, making him wealthier than any other member of the society. This distribution clearly infringes the original pattern established in D1. Is D2 just? Is Chamberlain entitled to his money?

Yes, says Nozick. Since everyone in D1 was entitled to what he had, there is no injustice in the starting point that resulted in D2. The spectators who paid twenty-five cents in the move from D1 to D2 did so freely and therefore have no complaint. Nor do those who had no desire to watch Chamberlain, for they have lost nothing. *No injustice arises*. This demonstrates, in Nozick's view, the flaw in all *non-entitlement* theories of justice. They assume that it is a necessary condition for a just distribution that it contains a certain structure or fits a certain pattern. Nozick also contends that *any* pattern is destructive of freedom. To impose a pattern of distribution requires an intolerable level of coercion, denying individuals the right to employ their talents and labour as they see fit. Hence distributive justice, according to Nozick, far from requiring a redistribution of wealth, actually prohibits it. The minimal state is therefore the best method by which to secure distributive justice.

What if wealth is spread *unfairly*? That is not a problem for Nozick. 'If each person's holdings are just, then the total set (distribution) of holdings is just'. And that's that.

Locke, you will recall, argues that by mixing his labour with natural resources, a person can convert common property into private property. For Nozick, there is a limit to this; a person may acquire it only 'at least where there is enough, and as good, left in common for others'. One still has to share the pool of common property with others. As Nozick asks (rather presciently in view of the recent development of private space programmes): 'If a private astronaut clears a place on Mars, has he mixed his labor with (so that he comes to own) the whole planet, the whole uninhabited universe, or just a particular plot?'

Nozick adopts a form of this idea – the so-called 'Lockean proviso' – by arguing that I have a legitimate objection against your otherwise just acquisition if it fails to leave me with, in Locke's phrase, 'enough and as good'. This means that I may justly complain when your acquisition results in my being worse off. But I do not have a legitimate complaint, even if my welfare is reduced by a diminution in the property that remains available for me to acquire, if I am properly compensated for my loss by other effects of your conduct.

Why a state at all?

Nozick's aversion to an over-arching state would suggest that he's an anarchist. But he is at pains to demonstrate that he is not actually calling for the abolition of states in their entirety and is therefore not an anarchist. In a world without states, members would be forced to protect their own lives and property. Nozick believes that people would naturally unite to form voluntary protection associations, taking turns to keep an eye on each other's property and determining how offenders are to be punished. In time, a group will emerge that will set up a business providing security at a price. Others may wish to compete, by offering security at lower prices or by offering a superior service. The market would take care of the problem. Eventually, one large enterprise would materialize in which the anarchists had the greatest faith. Competition will inevitably give rise to other companies. With increased competition comes discord. Disputes may arise, which are likely to be settled by some form of agreed arbitration or mediation. You get the picture. What has emerged is a private organization that looks like a state, sounds like a state but is not a state. The 'invisible hand' of market forces has created a huge private firm whose dominant purpose is to protect and defend its clients.

What about individuals who do not wish to be part of this system and prefer to look after themselves and penalize those who infringe their rights? Nozick's agency or firm will not permit this. Indeed it is morally bound not to, because its *raison d'être* is to protect its clients, which entails that they have a right not to be arrested, prosecuted or punished unfairly or excessively. The firm must prohibit these independent individuals from acting against its clients. It will therefore administer justice to the extent that it protects its clients.

Doesn't this imply that the firm has adopted one of the essential roles of a state: a monopoly in respect of the legitimate use of force? It has morphed into what Nozick dubs an 'ultra-minimal state'. What of those 'independents' who are left out in the cold? They must be offered the same protection as clients enjoy, by compensating them for their exclusion. The ultra-minimal state will extend its protection to them, at a price. They will be charged the amount that they would have paid to defend themselves. Thus this nominal state will have assumed yet another state function: protecting all within its borders. The fee rendered is in effect a tax but because it is paid voluntarily by clients and represents what non-clients would have paid anyway, it does not infringe Nozick's precious right of self-ownership. The ultra-minimal state is now transformed into a full-blown minimal state.

Unjust acquisitions

The initial acquisition of property is very often unjust. Think of the land taken centuries ago by colonists of numerous countries around the world. Property may be plundered, obtained by fraud or by force. It is obviously far easier to rectify an unjust acquisition by an individual than one by a foreign state. Yet even historical injustices, Nozick concedes, call for rectification. But how? The descendants of those who have been robbed of their land would seem to have a valid claim against those who benefited from the transgression. But how do we formulate a satisfactory method by which to compensate them?

Nozick rejects Rawls's difference principle, which argues that because *all* members of society benefit from social co-operation, the poor are automatically entitled to a share in the earnings of the more successful members. Instead, like Rawls, he proposes that the best that can be done is to adopt a 'rule of thumb' that maximizes the position of the least well-off: those who are likely to be worse off than they otherwise would have been but for the historical injustice. They would receive compensation from those who are likely to be better off than they otherwise would have been but for the historical injustice. This seems to be a concession to something like Rawls's difference principle. Is Nozick's apparent recognition of the need for a state, though limited, a damaging compromise? He, rather enigmatically, declares:

> Although to introduce socialism as the punishment for our sins would be to go too far, past injustices might be so great as to make necessary in the short run a more extensive state in order to rectify them.

This suggests that to secure justice, or at least to rectify historical wrongs, some coercive institution may be required.

Knocking Nozick

The numerous quarrels about Nozick's ideas provide a valuable tool by which to unlock some of the key assumptions that lie at the heart of his radical thesis. There are those – social democrats, for example – who spurn the materialism and avarice that the free market embodies. (I will return to this quandary in Chapter 9.) This accounts, in part, for the largely hostile reception of Nozick's book. Predictably, the strongest complaints emanated from those who conceive social justice as a means by which to equalize or reduce the inequities of wealth distribution in society. To them the rejection of redistribution or 'patterned' principles of fairness is inimical to the realization of an ideal social order.

Some find his refutation of utilitarianism unfounded. H.L.A. Hart describes it as paradoxical, because it yields an outcome that is indistinguishable from one of the least satisfactory implications of an absolute maximizing utilitarianism, in that 'given certain conditions there is nothing to choose between a society where few enjoy great happiness and very many very little and a society where happiness is more equally spread'. A utilitarian would regard the aggregate or average welfare in both societies as the same; Nozick treats the situation as historical. Neither, Hart seems to be claiming, is likely to disrupt the existing pattern of distribution, however unequal. Other critics accuse Nozick's compensation principle of exhibiting incipient utilitarianism! It would, they claim, if applied generally, undermine his libertarianism by tolerating invasion of rights to improve the lot of an affected individual. But, in the absence of his compensation principle, the minimal state could turn into Nozick's worst nightmare: a welfare state!

What about the practical prospects of establishing a minimal or night-watchman state? How does it materialize from a state of nature? Can it really do so without violating individuals' rights? How is the minimal state to be kept minimal? Who keeps watch over the watchman? How are the poor to be prevented from attaining political power? Can a minimal state avoid and relieve economic deprivation?

Few detractors regard Nozick's theory of historical entitlement with much enthusiasm. Any compulsory or involuntary transfers of property, you will recall, would encroach on the owner's rights. Any redistribution of property must therefore occur with the owners' consent. Nozick is willing to permit the historically original acquisition of property to endow the owner with absolute rights, which he may then transfer to the next owner. Nozick does not, as far as I can see, tell us on what *principle* this initial property right is secured. He does, as we have observed, embrace Locke's idea of ownership but the precise method by which the first owner accrues his right (a flag in the ground; an open pronouncement?) is left unclear.

It has been suggested that the concept of private ownership may actually *decrease* freedom. Think of the enclosure movement in eighteenth-century England; by statute, common land was 'enclosed', rendering it inaccessible to those who previously could enjoy it. The distressing consequences are vividly – and heartbreakingly – evoked by the poet John Clare (1793–1864) who, in his poem *The Moors*, laments that 'the sky-bound moors are all blocked where … [F]ence now meets fence in owners' little bounds'. Where 'the field was our church, and there were 'paths to freedom and to childhood dear/A board sticks up to notice "no road here" … Enclosure came and trampled on the grave/Of labour's rights and left the poor a slave'.

Nozick's comparison of taxation to forced labour has, not surprisingly, been assailed by several writers. It has also been argued that if our lives, as Nozick strongly proclaims, have moral value, then we need the *capacity* or opportunity to live them. I can hardly do that if I am afflicted by poverty; to live a fulfilling life I require the goods essential to give me a reasonable shot at this desirable objective. Nozick's system would surely deny me this capacity or 'capability'. This is the rallying cry of those who adopt a theory of justice based on this principle, as we shall next discover.

Summing up

Nozick's extreme form of libertarianism is based on the Lockean idea of entitlement: a distribution is just if everyone is *entitled* to the holdings they possess. But since some people will defraud others, or steal their property or oppress them, a principle of 'rectification' is required. His libertarianism also leads him to adopt a limited conception of the state as a 'night watchman', its role restricted to defence, security and judicial administration. The rest should be left to the private sector. The free market, he contends, is generally more efficient than the government. His analysis is based on moral, libertarian grounds, in particular the respect for individual rights.

7 Capability

What's the point of establishing principles of justice, and just institutions, if ordinary people lack the *capacity to enjoy* the rights and opportunities promised by these arrangements? The just society, as postulated by John Rawls's social contract, is an empty promise if people lack the ability to realize its undertakings. It is all very well endowing people with beneficial rights and interests, but these are empty unless they can be transformed into practical results. We should therefore 'concentrate on the actual behaviour of people, rather than presuming compliance by all with ideal behaviour'. These are the words of the Nobel Prize laureate Amartya Sen (1933–), who over a period of several decades has brought his extensive scholarship, Eastern and Western, economic and philosophical, to bear on the subject of justice. Others, notably the American philosopher Martha Nussbaum (1947–), have pursued a similar 'capabilities' approach. ('Capacity' might have been a less inelegant word).

This approach focusses on the lives people actually lead. Sen's point is that there is no single, perfectly just social arrangement that could win universal support. The concept of justice is more nuanced and complex. We need to recognize the limitations of an over-arching theory of justice à la Rawls and focus on the injustice suffered by millions on our planet, a subject we will return to in Chapter 12.

With its emphasis on personal welfare, health and general well-being, this multi-faceted approach appraises social measures and policies that advance social change. It accentuates the freedom that individuals *actually have* to do certain things and achieve certain objectives. Hence it attempts to treat people 'in the round' or holistically, seeking, as people do, a better life, health, education, social relationships and other elements of the 'good life'. This distinguishes its concerns from theories that concentrate wholly on subjective categories such as happiness or wealth. Consequently it is an approach that is espoused not only by philosophers but also by those engaged in development studies, welfare economics and social policy. It does not claim to offer an explanation for social injustices such as inequality, poverty and disease. Instead, it attempts to provide a conceptual footing for these factors. Reading their works, you will detect impatience with 'pure theory' and an aspirational desire to defeat the scourges of sickness, famine and other forms of misery that afflict so many people.

Freedom to do what?

Consider a disabled person who is unable to do certain things without help. Three situations could arise:

1. He has no help from anyone and is unable to leave his home.
2. He has a permanent helper provided by the state and is therefore able to leave his home whenever he wishes and move about freely.
3. He has well-paid servants who are required to obey his instructions and is therefore able to leave his home whenever he wishes and move about freely.

The capability approach asks the question: is he free to do what he wants? In case 1, he clearly lacks the capability to leave his home. Theories that define liberty not merely in respect of what a person is able to do but include the requirement that others *cannot remove that ability*, even if they wanted to, assume that the power arbitrarily to obstruct another's freedom to act as they wish exists, even if it is not actually exercised. This approach would regard the freedom of the disabled person as violated in both Case 1 and Case 2.

In Case 2 his liberty to leave his home depends on a social welfare arrangement that provides him with a helper. The capability approach, on the other hand, regards Case 1 as fundamentally different from the other two situations because it strips the person completely of his capability to leave his home. To treat Cases 1 and 2 as equivalent is to accept that establishing social security arrangements or a caring society has no impact on a disabled person's freedom. That would be a major hole in a theory of justice.

Critical to this approach is that if we want to create a just society, capabilities should be pursued for *every person*, treating them as an end and not merely as a means to some end. It rejects the utilitarianism implicit in, for example, determining the quality of life by reference to a country's per capita gross national product (GNP). This fails to reveal how income and wealth are actually *distributed*. Nor does the GNP reflect conditions that are not necessarily related to wealth, such as life expectancy, infant mortality, educational opportunities and other important features of a society. As we saw in Chapter 4, a utilitarian calculus is based on the accumulation of happiness or welfare. The capability approach, particularly as advanced by Nussbaum, is founded on the concept of the dignity of a human being, with a life worthy of that dignity, so as to enable a person to flourish. She identifies ten 'central human capabilities':

1. *Life*: the ability to live to the end of a human life of normal length.
2. *Bodily health*: the ability to enjoy good health, including reproductive health; to be adequately nourished; to have adequate shelter.
3. *Bodily integrity:* the ability to move freely from place to place; to be secure against violent assault, including sexual assault and domestic violence; having opportunities for sexual satisfaction and for choice in matters of reproduction.
4. *Senses, imagination and thought:* the ability to use the senses, to imagine, think and reason in a 'truly human' way, informed and cultivated by an adequate education, including literacy and basic mathematical and scientific training.
5. *Emotions:* the ability to have attachments to things and people outside ourselves; to love those who love and care for us, to grieve at their absence; to have one's emotional development not blighted by fear and anxiety.
6. *Practical reason:* the ability to form a concept of the good and to engage in critical reflection about the planning of one's life, which entails protection for liberty of conscience and religious observance.
7. *Affiliation:* the ability to live with and toward others, to recognize and show concern for other human beings, to engage in various forms of social interaction; to be able to imagine the situation of another; self-respect and non-humiliation; to be treated as a dignified being whose worth is equal to that of others.
8. *Other species*: the ability to live with concern for and in relation to animals, plants and the world of nature.
9. *Play:* the ability to laugh, to play, to enjoy recreational activities.
10. *Control over one's environment:* the ability to participate effectively in the political choices that govern one's life; having the right of political participation, protection of free speech and

> association and the ability to hold property and have property rights on an equal basis with others; to have the right to seek employment on an equal basis with others; the freedom from unwarranted search and seizure; to work as a human being, exercising practical reason and entering into meaningful relationships of mutual recognition with other workers.

Nussbaum's long inventory echoes the works of the eminent Catholic philosopher St Thomas Aquinas (1225–74), who was himself influenced by Aristotle's ethics. In his *Summa Theologiae*, Aquinas links Aristotle's ideas to the reconciliation of secular and Christian authority, contending that Christianity was a phase in the development of humanity that was unavailable to the Greeks. Reviving Aristotle's idea of political life of the *polis*, he regards the state as the natural and superior form of association, but one subordinate to divine guidance of the world. The *polis* in which we were destined to live was therefore, Nussbaum says, Christian. Natural law is 'participation' in the eternal law, the rational plan that governs creation. When we 'receive' natural law, it comprises the principles of practical rationality by which human action is to be judged as reasonable or unreasonable. They are binding because, as rational beings, we are directed towards them by nature; they steer us toward the good and several specific goods. Intuitively we understand what these goods are: they include life, knowledge, procreation, society and reasonable conduct. Like Aristotle, Aquinas believes that the good is prior to the right. Whether an act is right matters less than whether it achieves or is some good.

Aquinas's philosophy has its most compelling contemporary champion in John Finnis (1940–), who advances his ideas, along with those of Plato and Aristotle, to postulate seven 'basic forms of human flourishing' and nine 'basic requirements of practical reasonableness'. Human reason guides us how best to achieve our desires. Finnis starts with the Aristotelian question: *what constitutes a worthwhile, valuable, desirable life*? These are the 'basic forms of good':

1. *Life*. The drive for self-preservation we all have; includes health, freedom from pain and the procreation of children.
2. *Knowledge*. It is a good in itself to be well informed rather than ignorant or muddled.
3. *Play*. Recreation, enjoyment, fun.
4. *Aesthetic experience*. An appreciation of beauty in art or nature.
5. *Sociability (friendship)*. Acting in the interests of one's friends.
6. *Practical reasonableness*. Employing one's intelligence to solve problems or deciding what to do, how to live and shaping one's character.
7. '*Religion*'. Our concern about an order of things that transcends our individual interests.

In contrast to Nussbaum, Sen favours a more rounded, organic and less categorical description of capabilities, arguing that they depend on the context in which they arise. A good deal of Sen's analysis rests on the significance he attaches to the role of 'public reasoning' that encourages 'different voices', from diverse sections of the community, to be heard. The question remains of how freedom or human dignity is connected to the actual life people choose to lead. The argument then turns to what are called (again rather inelegantly) 'functionings'.

Functionings

What sort of things makes us what we are? More specifically, what do we *need* to function so as to enjoy a life worthy of human dignity? The capabilities approach employs the term functionings to describe 'beings and doings': the various conditions and actions of a person. 'Beings' includes being properly fed on the one hand or malnourished on the other; living in a satisfactory environment or sleeping rough; being educated or illiterate; being a law-abiding citizen or a criminal and so on. 'Doings' comprise caring for children, travelling, voting, debating, drug-taking, hunting and so on.

From these examples we can draw certain conclusions. The point is to demonstrate how numerous aspects of a person can be designated either as a 'being' or a 'doing'. These categories are morally neutral; they might be good (being healthy) or bad (being assaulted), although in some cases their moral quality is *contextual.* A mother caring for her child looks, on the face of it, to be a positive functioning. But a feminist might regard it as negative if the mother did not *choose* to undertake this responsibility in circumstances where society fails to protect equal opportunities and provides inadequate support for women in this position.

Our capabilities are therefore the genuine opportunities that we possess to achieve functionings. For example, my travelling is a functioning, my concrete prospect of travelling is my matching capability. What I achieve, on the one hand, and the genuine freedom I have to choose, on the other. Someone may decide to fast to improve his health. This is very different from the situation of a person who is suffering from starvation. Both are deprived of food but the circumstances of that deprivation are completely different. Each 'functioning' has an effect on an individual's well-being, but the first is obviously a deliberate choice, the second is not. When comparing their respective welfare, the fact that the second lacks the capability to feed himself is an essential criterion.

Starving or sleeping rough is a functioning; it is not normally the exercise of a choice. A person's well-being is contingent on how his mode of living arose. To put it in the language of the capabilities approach, the combination of my functionings indicates my tangible accomplishments; my capabilities embody my freedom to choose between alternative combinations of functionings.

What does this all add up to? And what does it have to do with justice? The thrust of the argument is that by evaluating your 'functionings' and 'capabilities' you can most effectively measure the extent to which you are free to pursue those activities that you prize and thereby to become the person you want to be. Your beings and doings comprise what makes your life worthwhile. But to explore the different functionings available to people we need to adopt a comprehensive approach; this means we must enquire which combination of capabilities is genuinely available to a person. I may want to be a breadwinner and a good parent. Can I do both?

The theory enables us to test government policy to see whether it affects people's capabilities and functionings. For example, we might ask whether people can enjoy good health if they have no access to clean drinking water, be healthy without sufficient food, be secure without good government or function effectively without a good education?

The capabilities approach is *outcome-oriented*. Unlike social contractarianism, it looks to the actual content of an outcome to see whether it appears to be compatible with a life that affords human dignity and creates a more just society. It is therefore able to offer a richer, more nuanced and more compassionate account of human needs. Nussbaum stresses that we must recognize the needs of the sick, the elderly, the disabled and of other species. (This aspect of justice is considered in Chapter 10.) The approach argues that where a society accepts that there is a serious deficit in people's capabilities, justice demands that it makes every effort to rectify that deficiency instead of attempting to compensate the 'victims' financially.

One of the mainsprings of this logic is dissatisfaction with what it perceives to be a one-dimensional analysis of human needs. The concentration on 'normal' human beings of thinkers such as Rawls's results in the neglect of the diversity of people with respect to their abilities, race, religion and so on, although

Rawls does endorse the requirement for 'special needs' including for those who live with a disability. The capability approach attempts to remedy this failure by acknowledging the manifold forms of functionings and capabilities. It does this by extending the evaluation of individuals' welfare to incorporate factors that are often overlooked. For example, the well-being of a woman turns not merely on the degree to which she suffers discrimination at work but includes other elements, such as the quality of her relationships and the support and care she receives. The assessment of the position of women in society is multi-pronged and requires a more complex analysis, a matter we will return to in Chapter 10.

Conversions

A wealthy person may acquire the latest, most advanced mountain bike to pursue his sport. But the brand or design of a bicycle is of little significance to a poor person who just needs to get to work on time. This feature contributes to a functioning: mobility; a particular resource is thus transformed into a functioning. Sen demonstrates how this factor extends both to marketable goods and services and to those that materialize from the non-market economy to which people are attracted. The relation between a commodity, on the one hand, and the achievement of certain beings and doings, on the other, is described as a 'conversion factor'. This explains the degree to which a person is able to convert a resource into a functioning. For example, a high conversion factor would be attributed to a person who learnt to ride a bicycle as a child, because he can effortlessly transform his bicycle into a means of mobility. The conversion factor of a disabled person, however, would be low, because he is able to obtain no or limited functioning (mobility) from his bicycle.

Conversion factors vary according to their source. Certain factors are peculiar to a specific individual; this may include their physical condition, intelligence or sex. Society may influence your conversion factors. These might comprise, for instance, public attitudes and policies with regard to discrimination, welfare support and other social norms. Even environmental factors could limit or enhance your ability to convert your possessions into a functioning: a bicycle is of limited practical use on poorly maintained roads and perhaps even dangerous if you ride in polluted air. Sen contends that 'capability' signifies not merely one's ability to do something but also the prospect of turning an opportunity into reality, circumscribed by various personal, social and environmental conversion factors.

Is it really a theory of justice?

The approach has stimulated several significant practical applications, especially some developed by the United Nations. It has provided a valuable alternative – the so-called Human Development Index (HDI) – to the conventional metrics of Gross Domestic Product (GDP) and GNP to measure levels of development in societies. The HDI incorporates factors such as life expectancy, adult literacy and school enrolment to identify the degree of poverty, inequality and other capability deficiencies that can exist even in a country with high GDP. Other applications have been developed by the UN to assess gender inequality, such as the Gender Empowerment Measure (GEM) and the Gender Inequality Index.

It is clear that the capability approach offers not only a credible alternative to utilitarian and other distributive standpoints, but also a practical barometer of capabilities and their insufficiency. To what extent, however, can it be called a theory of justice? This question is complicated by the fact that there is no single capability approach. There are numerous versions and applications and, as you might expect, a fair amount of disagreement among capability scholars.

Sen's analysis has been criticized for 'under-theorising' the concept of justice. He appears to be willing to accept this reproach, preferring to assign importance to the fact that his account both improves the prospects for justice and for removing injustice across the globe. Nussbaum, however, seeks to provide a more philosophical foundation. This embraces, as we have seen, a concept of human dignity associated with human flourishing in the Aristotelian sense. She therefore resists the claim that the approach is 'under-theorized', though her analysis does not really constitute a comprehensive theory of justice; indeed, she describes it as 'a partial and minimal account of social justice'. But, while she postulates a catalogue of capabilities that all governments should guarantee, and concentrates on the minimum standard to be achieved, she does not consider what the actual requirements of justice are once these standards have been met. She rejects any attempt to impose a universal theory that would apply to all societies.

Sen, as we saw, repudiates the need for a 'canonical' check-list of capabilities, selected by theorists in the absence of public reasoning, and therefore finds it difficult to accept Nussbaum's enumeration. He, on the other hand, has been reproached for his alleged paternalism in imposing or assuming a particular form of the good life. Another adherent of the capability approach, Ingrid Robeyns (1972–), resists any endeavour to prescribe a particular catalogue of capabilities to be applied across the board. She proposes instead a procedural method to choose a list of appropriate capabilities for specific purposes, such as appraising gender inequality in terms of capabilities.

Their quarrel with Rawls is not entirely convincing. His social contract is treated as if it were an actual, rather than hypothetical, agreement between the people in the original position. But it was conceived as an ideal, a heuristic tool by which to specify the principles of justice that those stripped of their identities would choose. Sen and his followers build a powerful case for promoting justice at grassroots level. This engenders hostility to a Rawlsian approach on two main grounds: the social contract is regarded as both transcendental and hypothetical, and it allegedly neglects the importance of reasoned public discussion and agreement on the principles of justice. But these elements strike me as inevitable features of any social contractarian approach. Moreover, isn't this comparing apples and oranges? Rawls proffers an *ideal* theory of justice; the capability approach steers the debate towards the practical or empirical. Rawls's theory specifies the just *institutions* needed in a *liberal democratic state* to protect individual *citizens*. The capability approach is considerably more ambitious, extending to all human beings wherever they live and to general social norms and conventions, not merely institutions.

Needless to say, Rawlsian theorists have numerous complaints in return. They dislike the presupposition of a specific ethical position that the capability approach adopts. Nor is there sympathy for its public concept of justice entailing the provision of information on which claims of injustice can be made. Rawlsians insist that social stability requires a common standard of the principles of justice. Capabilities cannot, they contend, be easily evaluated or calculated in this public manner, and so the capability approach is not a practicable theory of justice. Like Ronald Dworkin (whose ideas I discuss in Chapter 9), I am unable to see why Rawlsian principles of justice cannot be successfully deployed to resolve problems in 'the real world'. Nor is it obvious, as Sen claims, that public reasoning about the ranking of capabilities offers a means by which to identify these problems without a general theory to recommend how these diverse opinions should be assessed in relation to a real-world judgement about a contentious question. I shall return to consider some of these challenging matters in the context of the wider problems of global justice in Chapter 12.

Summing up

At the core of the capability approach to justice is the idea that the chance to attain well-being is a moral imperative. Everyone should have the opportunity to achieve the best for themselves. This freedom is a function of individuals' capabilities: their actual opportunities to do and be what they regard as valuable. It attempts to evaluate personal well-being and social arrangements and to develop policies that advance social change, including the 'human development approach'.

8
Justice and the free market

What if justice had nothing to do with the fair distribution of wealth or its redistribution as proposed, for example, by Rawls? For him, 'all social values – liberty and opportunity, income and wealth and the social bases of self-respect – are to be distributed equally unless an unequal distribution of any, or all, of these values is to everyone's advantage'. But why not simply allow the liberty of an open, free market to determine what is just?

This chapter considers the idea that free and unfettered markets are a requirement of social justice. In the previous chapter, we saw how some theorists, such as Robert Nozick, subscribe to the idea that the free exchange of goods and services between autonomous individuals, unconstrained by the state, is the key to a just society. Their argument is based on the importance of allowing individuals to participate in voluntary exchange; this respects their liberty and promotes fairness. Moreover, the free market, they maintain, advances both the efficiency and the general welfare of the community.

Protecting the rights of individuals to engage freely in the market is an important feature of a capitalist society that engenders justice for all. Can this be true?

What is a free market?

A free market is based on the economic conditions of supply and demand, with little or no government interference or control. Each exchange or transaction is a voluntary agreement between the parties. In practice, governmental intervention is inevitable to impose taxes, control prices and competition.

Chief among the most influential theorists who are associated with free markets is the Scottish philosopher Adam Smith (1723–1790), who is celebrated as the originator of economic theory. Later economists, such as Thomas Malthus (1766–1834) and his friend David Ricardo (1772–1823), developed his ideas which, in turn, were most prominently advanced in the twentieth century by Joseph Schumpeter (1883–1950) and F.A. von Hayek (1899–1992) and the so-called 'Chicago School', with the Nobel laureate, Milton Friedman (1912–2006) as its most illustrious member.

Some claim that the free market promotes general welfare. When they do, they generally adopt, in effect, the utilitarian view that a rational person always chooses to do what will maximize his satisfactions. And if he wants something badly enough, he will be prepared to *pay* for it. They sometimes also rely on the fact that markets protect individuals' liberty or rights to use their goods as they please, to buy and sell freely.

Some free market theorists support the idea advanced by Adam Smith, that what he called the 'invisible hand' of the market generates efficiency which, in turn, advances general welfare and economic growth. This, of course, neglects the problem of *distribution* of wealth. Does a laissez faire market actually improve the condition of the least well-off? Is there really a 'trickle-down effect' that benefits the underprivileged? Other market devotees look to the consequences of economic freedom: markets encourage rationality, which in turn contributes to virtue and enlightened values. Another view commends the effect markets have on distribution: they reward hard or unsociable work, giving people what they deserve.

Opponents of the free market have long condemned its operation as excessively materialistic. Rousseau, Karl Marx (1818–1883) and Friedrich Engels (1820–1895) are among the prominent adversaries of market forces and their impact on the poorer members of society. The main alternative – at least until the collapse of communism in Russia and Eastern Europe – was a so-called command economy, centrally planned and normally requiring an authoritarian government. A more moderate, less oppressive, substitute was championed by the likes of John Stuart Mill and the economist John Maynard Keynes (1843–1946), whose views have influenced social democratic movements, especially in Europe. John Rawls may, of course, be counted among those who seek political and institutional curbs on what a former British prime minister once described as the 'unpleasant and unacceptable face of capitalism'.

Free marketeers have much in common with utilitarians who seek to demonstrate how the operation of market forces secures the welfare of its participants. In particular, they trust 'Pareto efficiency', named after the Italian economist Vilfredo Pareto (1848–1923). This is attained when at least one person is better off and no one is made worse off. For example, suppose that I am willing to sell you my car for £1,000. You estimate its worth as £2,000 but are content to pay me £1,500, which I am happy to accept. We are both better off and neither of us is worse off. A different outcome, called 'Pareto optimality', describes a situation where at least one person is worse off. It occurs when an economy is perfectly competitive and in a state of equilibrium. Prices therefore reflect the values of the market. If a unit of goods or services could generate more satisfaction in an activity other than its present one, somebody would have been prepared to pay more for it and it would therefore have been attracted to the new use. Free-market champions like what they call a 'Pareto-superior' outcome because it generates a morally superior result.

The reality is that this seldom happens. In practice, no economy can be expected to attain the Pareto Optimality. There is usually a loser. Nor does it offer a useful policy tool, as it is seldom possible to make someone better off without making someone else worse off. The market contains all kinds of imperfections: monopolies, lack of information, transaction costs and so on. In fact, transaction costs are often ignored when assessing the extent of a trader's profit. For example, I sell my first-rate Chianti for €20 per litre. You find a similar wine being sold by a vineyard for only €15. You will be tempted to buy the cheaper product, regarding my profit as too high. But you are likely to forget the expenses the transaction generated; these include my information costs (finding a supplier), bargaining costs, enforcement costs (protecting myself against my supplier breaching his contract) and regulatory costs (complying with European Union regulations, insurance costs and so on).

An improvement of this calculation was developed by two British economists, Nicholas Kaldor (1908–1986) and the Nobel Prize laureate John Hicks (1904–1989). The so-called Kaldor-Hicks test, which they formulated, is satisfied when the alteration in the allocation of resources produces sufficient money to recompense the losers. In other words, any gains made ought to be enough, in theory, to permit those who benefit to *compensate* those who do not.

Does the free market really produce justice?

This is not a straightforward question; economies are partly a function of individual preferences, which are subject to change.

More importantly, the 'players' are far from equal: the opportunity for the powerful to exploit the weak is always present: large corporations are often accused of driving smaller companies out of business. Critics of capitalism point to the perpetual centralisation and concentration of production and ownership. In the process, larger companies overpower or acquire their smaller rivals. The larger the corporation, the more inexpensively it can purchase its supplies and utilities and transport its goods. It is also able to obtain credit more easily, enabling it to expand when the economy is strong and survive when it is weak. Research and development, marketing and political influence facilitate its power over competitors. It is also in a stronger position to enlist the services of lawyers, tax advisers and, as we have recently seen, tax havens.

What about the effects of external forces? The vaunted efficiency that markets create often relates to the satisfaction of individuals' desires, but these may be manipulated by advertising or other social pressure. The Coase theorem (see next page) claims that these effects may be avoided by bargaining. But this is not always easy in the real world of competing interests. This is why the free market is often criticized, for example by Marxists and communitarians, who blame it for creating divisions in society by promoting materialism and self-interest.

Is a 'free' market genuinely free? Most societies impose varying degrees of legal and regulatory restraints on its independence; certain things cannot be bought and sold. Selling babies, one's organs and commercial surrogacy are widely prohibited, or at least legally controlled. Anti-trust laws are designed to curtail monopolies. The promotion of ethical business practices, improved corporate governance, anti-corruption legislation, consumer protection and the recognition of trade union rights are among the many initiatives that are intended to curb the excesses of market forces, abuse and exploitation.

THE COASE THEOREM

A factory emits smoke that damages laundry hung outdoors by five nearby residents. Each resident suffers £75 in damages, a total of £375. Two possible corrective measures could prevent the smoke damage: either a smoke-screen could be installed on the factory's chimney, at a cost of £150, or each resident could be provided with an electric tumble drier at a cost of £50. The *efficient* solution is clearly to install the smoke-screen, as it eradicates damage totalling £375 for a disbursement of only £150, and it is cheaper than purchasing five electric driers for £250.

The question raised by Coase is whether the efficient outcome would result if the *right to clean air* were given to the residents or if the *right to pollute* is given to the factory. In the case of the former, the factory has three choices: pollute and pay £375 in damages, install a smoke-screen for £150 or buy five tumble driers for the residents at a total cost of £250. The factory would, naturally, install the smoke-screen: the efficient solution. If there is a right to pollute, the residents have three choices: suffer their collective damages of £375, buy five driers for £250 or buy a smoke-screen for the factory for £150. They, too, would choose to buy the smoke-screen.

The efficient outcome would therefore be achieved *regardless of the assignment of the legal right*. This simple hypothesis assumes that the residents would incur no costs in coming together to negotiate with the factory. Coase calls this *'zero transaction costs'*. The real world is unfortunately more complicated; some costs would inevitably be incurred.

The Coase theorem, in its simple form, is: where there are zero transaction costs, the efficient outcome will occur regardless of the choice of legal rule.

But the question remains whether economic liberty advances the cause of *justice*. It presumes an *initial* distribution of wealth that may be totally *unjust*. Creating an efficient society may lead to existing inequalities being maintained. Is wealth maximization a value that is worth trading off against justice? Does increasing social wealth morally improve society? Is the satisfaction of individual wants an ethical index of social welfare?

Two illuminating examples are cited by Michael Sandel to demonstrate the unsatisfactory impact of the market on non-business transactions. One involves an affluent couple, the Sterns, who were unable to conceive a child. They signed a contract with a young working-class mother, Mary Beth, under which she agreed to be artificially inseminated with Mr Stern's sperm, bear the child and hand it over to the Sterns at birth. She also undertook to waive her maternal rights so that Mrs Stern could adopt the baby. In return, she would receive $10,000 on delivery, plus her medical expenses. After the child was born, Mary Beth declined to part with it and fled to another state where she was apprehended by the police. Under the terms of a court order, the child was returned to the Sterns.

The custody dispute came before a court. Leaving aside the legal issue, Professor Sandel asks what the morally correct outcome is. A strict application of market principles would support the enforcement of the contract, although it is arguable whether Mary Beth's consent was based partly on her difficulty in predicting how she would feel once she had given birth to the baby. Financial considerations may also have clouded her judgement. More fundamentally, is it acceptable to create a market in babies? Does this not transform babies into commodities and exploit women by treating pregnancy as a commercial enterprise?

The judge upheld the contract. He held it was made by equal parties, each of whom had what the other desired. Nor, he ruled, was surrogacy baby-selling; Mr Stern did not buy the baby from Mary Beth, he paid her to carry his child to term. It was his biological baby and he could not purchase what was already his. It was a contract of service. The judge compared it to sperm donation: if men are free to sell their sperm, women should be permitted to sell their reproductive capacity.

Matters did not end there. Mary Beth successfully appealed against the decision. The higher court unanimously reversed the trial judge's decision and declared the surrogacy contract void.

Nevertheless, it awarded custody of the child to the Sterns on the grounds that it was in its best interests. Mary Beth was, however, declared to be the child's legal mother. Why did the appeal succeed? First, because the mother's consent was not voluntary; she was 'irrevocably committed' before she knew her feelings for the baby. Second, she was influenced by the fear of being sued for breach of contract and, given her modest means, by the lure of the $10,000 fee. Indeed, the court remarked that it is only poorer women who would be likely to become surrogates. But the court sounded a more portentous note: 'There are in a civilized society', it affirmed, 'some things that money cannot buy'. The agreement was, to all intents and purposes, the sale of a child or, at least, the sale of a mother's right to her child. The transaction was encouraged by the fertility clinic for the profit that permeated and governed the deal.

The other intriguing case raises the question whether it is fairer for the army to conscript soldiers or hire them as it were on the open market. Libertarians oppose conscription because it is coercive and, some might argue, tantamount to slavery. Even utilitarians have reservations because the system restricts freedom of choice and therefore reduces general happiness. Both are likely to prefer a volunteer, market-based army. But, asks Sandel, is this market solution fair? And does it advance civic virtue and the common good? He queries whether this market is ever truly fair. We need to delve into the background of the volunteers: do they enjoy equal opportunity or are they driven to volunteer as a result of economic deprivation? The United States' military has a disproportionately high number of people from less well-off circumstances. The apparent freedom of choice exercised by volunteers is spurious. And serving in the military, like jury service, promotes civic virtue and responsibility. We should eschew the idea of treating soldiers as mercenaries. They ought to be considered to be performing a civic obligation that should be shared by all able-bodied people.

The rationale behind these conclusions is Sandel's communitarian opposition to the operation of the market. We shall consider this further in Chapter 11. He adds several other examples, including the outsourcing of military service and the interrogation of prisoners to private contractors, the trade in organs, cash rewards for pupils in underachieving schools and the sale of citizenship to immigrants. These questions are not merely about utility and consent, they are also 'about the right way of valuing key social practices ... [M]arketizing social practices may corrupt or degrade the norms we want to protect from market intrusion'.

These are cogent arguments, although the degree to which market forces spill into these realms is more striking in the United States and other advanced societies. Yet, as Sandel's examples show, US law did apply the brake to the commercialization of the surrogacy contract and there is palpable public unease in regard to the other instances of commodification that he mentions. Certainly, the sale of human organs is unlawful in every country, with the exception of Iran.

Summing up

The argument that justice is best achieved by the operation of a free market is highly controversial. Its devotees claim that it supports and safeguards a number of liberal values (including individual rights, limited government, equal justice under the law and property rights). Its critics and detractors point to the dangers of unrestrained competition (including monopolies, price-fixing and the corrosive social effects of the profit motive). It is often noted that governments are compelled to intervene to restrict market forces by, for instance, anti-trust legislation. Moreover, there are several social injustices that may be beyond the market's capacity to achieve. These are the subject of the next chapter.

9

Equality

Treating people as equals has long been regarded as a defining feature of justice. Progressive political movements frequently deploy the concept of equality as a rallying cry in their quest for a more just society. Discrimination on the grounds of race, religion, belief, age, disability or sexual orientation flies in the face of our contemporary notions of fairness and justice. In the political sphere, it is argued that access to participation should be distributed equally. To realize this objective, social institutions ought to be designed so that those who are under a disadvantage, whether economic, physical or another detriment, have an equal opportunity to take part in the democratic process.

Similarly, social equality requires that those who share comparable abilities ought to have roughly the same chances to attain employment or position, regardless of their economic or social class. Jobs should be given to those who are best-qualified, not on the basis of influence or social position. As far as justice is concerned, the central question is whether, and if so how much, the state ought to equalize social circumstances by redistributing wealth through taxation or by creating greater equality in the provision of welfare, health and education.

What is equality?

On the face of it, equality seems a reasonably straightforward idea, yet it is not always easy to define nor to demonstrate its connection with justice. It has been suggested that 'equality' has no single meaning, that it is inherently vague or even devoid of meaning. The term is used in a wide variety of senses. The concept of *moral equality* consists of the idea that, as a matter of morality, every person is entitled to equal concern and respect. It is based on the notion that, although we are not all exactly the same, we share certain essential characteristics and therefore we are equally worthy of dignity. But what exactly does this entail? When it comes to applying this idea in practice there is a distinction between *formal equality* and *substantive equality*. Formal equality consists of treating like cases alike: where the circumstances relating to different persons are the same, they ought, as a matter of justice, to be treated equally. Everyone is entitled to equal rights and subject to equal duties. Substantive equality goes beyond the matter of similarities and differences between people; it seeks to uncover the *basis* of these factors to determine whether they are relevant to differential treatment. It therefore attempts to expose the social, political and economic *forces* that give rise to discrimination and that require government to take action to reduce or eradicate inequality. Substantive equality plays an important role in many countries whose law and policy contains equality and non-discrimination provisions.

A dramatic instance of the judicial recognition of the principle of equality is the famous 1954 decision of the United States Supreme Court in *Brown v Board of Education of Topeka*. This declared that racial segregation in schools was unconstitutional and violated the Equal Protection Clause of the Fourteenth Amendment. In the words of Chief Justice Earl Warren: 'In the field of public education, the doctrine of "separate but equal" has no place. Separate educational facilities are inherently unequal'.

VOTES FOR WOMEN

New Zealand was the first country in the world to permit women to vote. Saudi Arabia, on the other hand, is the most recent. Vatican City is now the only state in which men but not women are enfranchised; only Cardinals (who are always male) may vote, for instance, for a new Pope. Some countries have been slower than others:

1893	New Zealand
1902	Australia
1906	Finland
1913	Norway
1915	Denmark
1917	Canada
1918	Austria, Germany, Poland, Russia
1919	The Netherlands
1920	The United States
1921	Sweden
1928	Britain, Ireland
1931	Spain
1934	Turkey
1944	France
1945	Italy
1947	Argentina, Japan, Mexico, Pakistan
1949	China
1950	India
1954	Colombia
1957	Malaysia, Zimbabwe
1962	Algeria
1963	Iran, Morocco
1964	Libya
1967	Ecuador
1971	Switzerland
1972	Bangladesh
1974	Jordan
1976	Portugal
1989	Namibia
1990	Western Samoa
1993	Kazakhstan, Moldova
2005	Kuwait
2006	United Arab Emirates
2011	Saudi Arabia

This ringing endorsement of the fundamental value of equality remains a central principle of American constitutional law.

Another aspect of equality, which we touched on in Chapter 2, is the idea of *proportional equality*. Aristotle claims that when people are unequal in relevant respects, to treat them equally is actually unjust. Justice requires that they be treated in proportion to their particular circumstances; they are therefore being treated equally.

Distinctions are also drawn between *equality of opportunity* and *equality of outcome*. Equality of opportunity is proposed to ensure that persons are given a *share* in goods, not merely a chance to acquire them without impediments. It normally describes fair competition for employment, education, housing and other positions or services and seeks to eliminate unfair discrimination. Equality of outcome, on the other hand, refers to a situation in which people enjoy roughly the same degree of prosperity or similar economic circumstances. This inevitably requires some form of redistribution of wealth from the rich to the poor.

Strong or weak equality?

Yet another elaboration is the distinction between equality in either a strong or weak sense. The philosopher Sir Bernard Williams describes a *strong* sense of equality, which is contained in the abstract claim that we are all born equal, and a *weaker* sense, the idea that we are equal because we share a 'common humanity'. He distinguishes between the *factual* claim that all men are equal and the *normative* claim that they should be *treated* as equal. But, he points out, both claims might be seen as problematic because they are either too strong or too weak. It is too strong to claim that we are all equal in our talents or abilities; we aren't. And it is too weak to assert that we are all human; it is true but inconsequential. Nevertheless, he regards this weak interpretation as politically important and non-trivial because it captures our common features: feeling pain, communicating, expressing affection and so on.

This raises the question of whether this *descriptive* claim supports a *prescriptive* one. In other words, does the fact that we are equal mean that we should be *treated* equally? Unequal treatment may be justified in the case, for example, of people with disabilities (whose needs are different) or in pursuing a policy of affirmative action. In the case of the 'too strong' interpretation, Williams, while conceding that we do not have equal ability (most of us lack the talents of Pavarotti or Einstein), asks whether we have an equal capacity to be *moral*: to distinguish right from wrong, good from bad. He thinks we do.

Against equality

You will recall that there are right-wing libertarians, such as Nozick (discussed in Chapter 6), who oppose equality on the ground that it requires government intervention to create social equality. But there are also anti-egalitarians on the left who argue that it is morally wrong to treat people as equal. They claim that equality is a '*comparative*' value; justice requires improving people's lives as an *absolute*. We shouldn't be *comparing* John's life with Jane's. Our moral duty, they say, is to reduce the suffering of the least advantaged. What matters is not that everyone should have *the same but* that all should have *enough*. If that can be achieved, it is immaterial whether some have greater wealth than others.

Another doubt is expressed by those who, while they value equality, question whether the focus on egalitarianism is the best way to achieve social justice. The philosopher Derek Parfit (1942–) prefers to concentrate on the plight of the weakest and poorest members of society, arguing that the greater people's deprivation, the more they deserve help: the worst-off should have priority over the better-off. This view, known as 'prioritarianism', claims that such a practice actually increases equality by creating an absolute or non-comparative standard that applies to everyone. Advocates of this view are concerned less with distribution than with helping the poor.

Parfit challenges the view held by so-called '*intrinsic* egalitarians' who regard equality as desirable even when it would not assist the individuals affected, for example, when equality can only be created by reducing the level of everyone's life. He concedes that equality may be *instrumentally* valuable; that encouraging equality helps to achieve other worthy ends. But he opposes the idea that equality is good *in itself*. An egalitarian, on the other hand, would claim that we cannot escape the comparative nature of distributive justice.

There are other objections to the pursuit of equality. First, some claim that a rigid, equal distribution between individuals fails to acknowledge their diversity: as we have different needs and desires, why should everyone receive the same? Surely, a person who is ill, it is argued, differs in his needs from a healthy individual? Simple equality erodes freedom and the distinct characteristics of individuals are neglected. Second, while it is claimed that we have a right to respect for our individual needs, we also have a duty to assume responsibility for our actions. This means that while we are entitled to compensation for inequalities that are not our fault, we should be held responsible for inequalities arising from the choices we freely exercise. This objection (which emphasizes our subjective expectations and obligations) leads many egalitarians to prefer equality of opportunity to equality of outcome: they support the idea that all should have an equal opportunity to attain the resources or prosperity they seek rather than insisting on everyone being treated as if they were the same.

The philosopher Peter Westen (1943–) famously argues that equality is an 'empty idea'. He criticizes the concept on a number of grounds; in particular, he claims that 'equality' is really about the *right* that people have to be treated equally if they are alike. Equality is often, he says, confused with rights. The idea of equality, he claims, cannot tell you how much of a particular good a person is entitled to, nor whether he has a particular right. Furthermore, equality cannot require that the state treats us all the same because it may treat us differently when there is a legitimate reason to do so. The celebrated maxim 'treat like cases alike' is meaningless, he says, because the central question is always: which cases are like what others in some relevant sense? Westen contends that statements about equality are tautologies; they are indistinguishable from claims about distributive justice. His premise is that while we share certain characteristics, people are not alike in every respect. Thus the concept of equality is *circular*: it tells us to treat like people alike; but when we ask who 'like people' are, the answer is 'people who should be treated alike'. Hence equality is empty; it has no independent moral content. It tells us nothing about how we should act. It is therefore redundant. Equality may be reduced to a statement about justice and vice versa. Needless to say, the usefulness of the concept of equality has been robustly defended by several philosophers.

A further objection to simple equality is that it tends to be tested by reference to its *results,* ignoring the *intention* behind the act in question. For instance, the inequality of a particular society may be an unintended consequence of a failed, but moral, attempt to redistribute resources, or a result of an unjust pursuit of efficiency. Suppose, for example, that malaria is rife in a particular country. A section of the community suffers from this deadly disease; a clear symptom of inequality. The society may, however, be just. The failure to prevent the spread of the mosquitoes that cause the infection may be an unintended, but acceptable, consequence of what the society regards as a fair distribution of resources. Or perhaps the action taken to prevent or treat the disease may have been inadequate. If so, is this a consequence of a political or moral decision to, for example, improve efficiency? In other words, equality of *results* is too restricted a test by which to determine whether a society is equal. We need, the argument goes, to know more about the moral quality of the choices that produced the result, especially the intention of those who made the decisions in question.

It is alleged, especially by feminists, that strict equality may promote uniformity rather than diversity. As we shall see in the next chapter, a fundamental principle of feminist theory is that sex is a variable relation of power and domination. This is also true in respect of race. These differences are frequently regarded as signifying diverse values. Women, and members of racial minorities, often look to the ideal of equality as an answer to the discrimination and oppression they suffer. But feminists and others argue that equality often seeks to deny these differences and hence it is not necessarily the solution to the problem. It may result in the assimilation of the very models of whiteness or maleness that caused the discrimination in the first place. We should, they argue, avoid conceiving of everyone as the same and instead celebrate diversity. Equality is important but not at the cost of overlooking or undermining diversity.

Utilitarianism, equality of welfare and resources

As we saw in Chapter 4, in calculating the greatest happiness of the greatest number, utilitarians treat every person as an equal unit. As everyone counts as one and no one as more than one and individual circumstances are disregarded, is it not a theory that endorses perfect equality? According to its critics, the answer is no. The theory fails to secure an equal outcome because it gives equal weight to *all* desires, including selfish needs and what Ronald Dworkin calls 'external' preferences (which I shall explain in a moment). Utilitarianism fails to capture what we normally understand by equality. Can I really expect others to subsidize my taste for expensive wine at the expense of their needs? Surely equality requires that a person cannot be deprived of resources to fund the costly needs of another. Equal treatment means that everyone has a right to a fair portion, rather than every interest weighing the same, however expensive its satisfaction may be. Utilitarianism is therefore criticized as lacking a means by which to distinguish between different preferences. It cannot be described as a theory that advances genuine moral equality, since it does not accord equal respect to every person.

Dworkin demonstrates this failure by differentiating 'personal' preferences from 'external' preferences. Personal preferences are things that I want for *myself*, as opposed to external preferences, which are things that I want for *others*. Dworkin claims that when we pursue the improvement of the general welfare, external preferences should be excluded because they weaken the fundamental political right of a 'basic right to equal concern and respect'. Any imposition of external preferences is tantamount to treating those on whom they are imposed as inferior, not to be treated as equals with equal concern and respect. This is the basis of his rejection of both utilitarianism and 'welfarism'. To use Dworkin's example, my *strong* personal preference for pistachio ice cream justifies society manufacturing pistachio. This is more persuasive than other reasons that may exist for *not* producing it (such as your *slight* preference for vanilla). But it is meaningless to speak of my *right* to have pistachio (or even my more general right to have my strong preferences satisfied) unless it implies that my preference justifies the production of pistachio even if the *collective* preferences of the community would be better served by producing vanilla. In other words, a political right exists only when the reasons for giving *me* what I want outweigh some *collective* justification that ordinarily affords a complete political defence of a decision.

A similar objection is made against *equality of welfare*, which is based on the idea that justice is served by securing equality in people's welfare. The problem here is that, like utilitarianism, it equates individual welfare with preference satisfaction. This means that all subjective preferences must be treated as equal. But I may want to harm you. Surely (as we discussed in Chapter 4) malevolent desires cannot be regarded as equal to benevolent ones. As in the case of expensive tastes, we are unlikely to accept that justice is served by granting individuals with a taste for vintage champagne more resources. Another problem with equality of welfare is that it disregards both the criterion of what people *deserve* and the extent to which individuals are personally responsible for their welfare.

These shortcomings may be avoided by *resource* equality, which treats people as responsible for their circumstances, except those that are beyond their control, such as their race, sex and intelligence. This approach argues that every individual is entitled to the same 'basic goods'. They are then free to use these as they please and may therefore increase their resources through the decisions they make. This is the position advanced by Rawls, whose principles of justice (as we saw in Chapter 5) permit inequalities, provided they are linked to offices and positions open to everyone under conditions of fair equality of opportunity. But they must also conform to the 'difference principle', which protects the interests of the least advantaged members of society. Equality is embodied in Rawls's first principle of justice. 'The minimum capacity for the sense of justice', he says, 'insures that everyone has equal rights … Equality is supported by the general facts of nature and not merely by a procedural rule …'

Equality is also a central value in other theories, including Sen's capability approach (discussed in Chapter 7) and the communitarian arguments for improving society in general that are the subject of Chapter 11. But the individualistic view of equality is most forcefully defended by Ronald Dworkin. Describing it as the 'sovereign virtue', his starting point is the principle of equal respect and concern to which all are entitled. To understand Dworkin's defence of equality, we need to explore certain features of his approach to justice, law and morals.

Rights as trumps

Dworkin presents a complex 'rights thesis' that argues for the prevalence of rights over concerns of the general welfare. The idea of 'rights as trumps' rests in part on the exclusion of 'external preferences' over 'personal preferences', as mentioned above. For him, most versions of utilitarianism fail to offer a satisfactory basis for the protection of individual rights. Only a limited form of utilitarianism, which disregards external preferences, provides some backing for the egalitarianism that is the main appeal of utilitarianism.

Equality is 'sovereign'

At the heart of Dworkin's theory is the principle that 'government must treat people as equals … [it] must impose no sacrifice or constraint on any citizen in virtue of an argument that the citizen could not accept without abandoning his sense of equal worth'. In *Sovereign Virtue*, he considers the sort of equality that a government should protect and sustain. Liberal egalitarianism ranks personal choice above individual luck:

> When and how far is it right that individuals bear disadvantages or misfortunes of their own situations themselves and when is it right, on the contrary, that others – the other members of the community in which

> they live, for example – relieve them from or mitigate the consequences of these disadvantages? … [I]ndividuals should be relieved of consequential responsibility for those unfortunate features of their situation that are brute bad luck but not from those that should be seen as flowing from their own choices.

This recognizes the importance of individual responsibility. We are permitted, in pursuit of a just society, to enquire *why* certain people are destitute. Some may be poor because they cannot find work. But what if they haven't tried to find employment and spend all day lounging? Do they deserve to benefit from the taxes levied on hard-working people? Dworkin argues that this would harm the concept of equality, which ought to allow the industrious to benefit and the idle to suffer the consequences of their indolence. He, not surprisingly, dismisses equality of welfare both because of the problem of deciding when individuals are at the same threshold of equivalence and also on the grounds that it offends any notion of justice to subsidize exotic tastes. To avoid this difficulty, he introduces the idea of personal responsibility as an element of his theory of equality. He distinguishes between 'option luck' (taking a deliberate risk, for example, in a casino) and 'brute luck' (being struck by lightning). The state may legitimately compensate those unfortunate to have been born with bad brute luck, such as a disability, but not those who have bad 'option luck', which is normally a consequence of independent choice. I can, and should, insure against the bad luck of my house being burgled. If I fail (as I confess I once did) I cannot complain if others are not taxed to compensate me for my loss. Justice does not require this.

Bad luck may afflict us from the moment of birth. Disability (discussed in Chapter 10) is a case in point. To address this problem, Dworkin asks us to imagine a hypothetical insurance policy; we know, more or less, what the reasonable prospects are for certain mishaps and misfortunes to occur and the availability, cost and value of medical and other remedies for the fallout from these instances of bad luck. We could then decide whether to insure against the possible misadventure. Taking all these decisions together we can calculate a hypothetical premium and a fair system of taxation. Some find the idea of responsibility too harsh, since it punishes those who are not to blame for their unhappy fate. But it does not entirely rule out special provisions being made for the disabled or gravely disadvantaged, even if pity rather than equality were the motivating factor.

RACE AND CRIMINAL JUSTICE

In the United States there is significant evidence to show that black men are more likely to be imprisoned than their white or Hispanic counterparts. Statistics collected by the US Bureau of Justice in 2014 found that black men have the highest imprisonment rate in every age group.

On 31 December 2014, there were 516,900 black male prisoners. They made up 37% of the male prison population, while white men made up 32% and Hispanic men 22%. At first glance, this might not seem like a significant difference but when you consider the demography of the whole country, it means 2.7% of all black men in the US are behind bars (2,724 per 100,000 black male residents). This contrasts with 1.1% of Hispanic men (1,091 per 100,000) and less than 0.5% of white men (465 prisoners per 100,000). Black men between the ages of 18 and 19 had a rate of imprisonment 10.5 times that of white men of the same age group.

Why?

Numerous explanations have been offered. Economic deprivation, lack of educational achievement, limited social mobility and deep-rooted prejudice are all implicated. Blacks and poor people are more often stopped and searched, especially for drugs. One study (Mauer and Cole, 2003) shows that although blacks and whites use and sell drugs at about the same rates, black men were almost 12 times more likely to be imprisoned than white men for this crime.

Equality versus liberty

It is often thought that equality can be achieved only at a cost for freedom. Those on the political right (conservatives) generally believe in *equality of opportunity*. They advocate a reduction in taxes and support initiatives and charities that help the unemployed to re-join the labour market, rather than helping them indefinitely. Conservatives believe that liberty requires minimal government interference. A person should be free to choose between being hugely wealthy or a homeless beggar. Liberals, on the other hand, positioned to the left of the political spectrum, tend to favour *equality of outcome*. They don't see wealth and poverty as purely a matter of choice and therefore champion higher taxes for the rich and greater help for the poor. Liberals generally support the idea that liberty requires protection against harm caused by others and that the government should enact and enforce laws that provide such protection. They are willing to permit the income of the very rich to be heavily taxed so that the poor can benefit from the money collected.

Dworkin always denied that there is a conflict between liberty and equality. As he puts it in his book, *Justice for Hedgehogs*, they are: 'not only compatible but intertwined'. He insists that liberty (including freedom of expression, religion and so on) is derived from the fundamental right to equality. He maintains that although a conflict may arise in some instances, in the case of equality of *resources*, basic liberties are actually a component of 'distributional equality' and are consequently routinely protected when equality is attained. Freedom is gained not at the expense of equality, but in the name of equality. Liberty and equality are, he argues, reconciled by either definitional or rational means.

What does he mean by 'definitional'? Central to Dworkin's notion of equality is the 'abstract egalitarian principle', which states that governments must improve people's lives and demonstrate equal concern for the lives of all individuals. The principle of egalitarianism entails the government respecting liberty because it obliges it to show equal concern for the lives of all those it governs. In other words, liberty derives not from some abstract right but from the right to equal concern and respect. By treating people equally it is, at the same time, upholding their liberty. Suppose a property developer decides to purchase land for housing that he will subsequently refuse to sell to black people. This would offend the fundamental egalitarian principle, because it does not treat all members of the community with equal concern. It is therefore necessary to impose a 'principle of independence' on the purchase, to place victims of prejudice in a position that closely resembles that which they would occupy if prejudice did not exist.

As we have seen, perfect or absolute equality is manifestly impossible. We are all different. My needs are not the same as yours. The best that we can strive for in a just society is to equalize, as far as possible, everyone's *opportunity* rather than to seek equality of *outcome*. We can attempt to advance opportunities for objective well-being (*equality of opportunity*), the satisfaction of subjective preferences (*welfare equality*) or of goods (*equality of resources*). Of the three, Dworkin champions equality of resources on the grounds that if we are all equal, why should you obtain more resources than me? Also, it is extremely difficult to measure my personal subjective 'welfare' needs against yours. The most appealing solution, as far as Dworkin is concerned, is to focus on equality of resources, since it generates a nice reconciliation of equality and liberty. Why? Because pursuing an equal distribution of resources permits people to determine what sort of lives they wish to live in the light of the effects their choices have on others and therefore on the total supply of available resources that they may legitimately use.

This distribution of resources implies an economic market, which Dworkin addresses by means of his hypothetical insurance market with a built-in 'envy test'. It calculates individuals' wishes by reference to the cost to others. Each person is detached from those features of his life caused by 'brute luck', such as aptitude and infirmity; only his *desires* count. We determine the cost to others by assuming each has security and the opportunity to develop his personality, free of prejudice. The key principle is that each be treated as equal. The free market must, in the name of liberty, be allowed to operate; it also respects the autonomy of individuals as equal moral persons.

This brief synopsis is a small section of Dworkin's kaleidoscopic vision of equality as it relates to justice. His thesis endorses the important idea that moral values are both independent and objective. Furthermore, we are all required to make our lives as good as possible; to live lives of 'dignity' that promote self-respect. And, of course, we have moral responsibilities towards others. By accepting the importance of self-respect, we are obliged, if we are to be logically consistent, to accept its significance not just in our own lives but also in the lives of others.

Although equality features in the capabilities approach (discussed in Chapter 7), its chief proponent, Amartya Sen, questions Dworkinian egalitarianism. Interestingly, like Dworkin, but unlike Sen, Nussbaum's approach is premised on the notion of human dignity. You will recall that at the core of Sen's analysis is the quest to understand the sources of capability deficits and inequity as a means of eliminating injustice. Thus *equality of capabilities* is central to his analysis. Sen is therefore highly critical of any theory of justice that is limited to the subject of equal *distribution* because it concentrates on *means*, instead of what individuals *acquire* from those means, that is ends. He declares that despite his 'immense admiration for Ronald Dworkin's work,' he rejects his accusation that the capability approach focuses on equality of *welfare*. No, says Sen, it is concerned with resources but only 'as a way of getting to equality of the capability to achieve'.

Another critic, G.A. Cohen (1941–2009), dislikes Dworkin's reliance on the free market to determine what constitutes a just distribution of wealth. He prefers the socialist idea that the purpose of equality is to enhance a person's needs 'for fulfilment in life'. It should, in other words, increase a person's 'potential for welfare', which presumably means that it should create an ethos that values caring for others. This seems a rather utopian ideal, notwithstanding the validity of his claim that the free market – which we shall now explore – is capable of producing injustice.

Summing up

As an ideal, equality looms large in most theories of justice. Inequalities are generally regarded as unjust, especially when they are the result of factors outside the control of people or groups. Egalitarians seek to improve the quality of life for the least advantaged. What constitutes equality, the precise conditions that require equalizing and how to remedy the injustices of inequality are all contentious issues.

10
Fraternity

In addition to treating people as equal (as discussed in the previous chapter) justice requires that we do not exclude those who might otherwise fall outside our realm of concern. Theories of justice – by accident or design – tend to focus on male, able-bodied, humans. They therefore exclude most inhabitants of our planet: women, the disabled and animals. But, in the spirit of fraternal respect, justice surely requires that duties are owed to members of each of these three groups. This chapter explores what these duties might be.

Women

Discrimination against women assumes numerous forms and persists around the world, despite the prohibition, by international human rights law, of discrimination on the basis of sex and the Convention on the Elimination of All Forms of Discrimination, which explicitly provides that states that have ratified the Convention must 'take all appropriate measures, including legislation, to modify or abolish existing laws, regulations, customs and practices which constitute discrimination against women'.

The law frequently relegates women and girls to second class status in regard to nationality and citizenship, education, marital rights, health, employment rights, parental rights, inheritance rights and property rights. Violence against women remains a serious problem. The law, culture or religion of several Islamic countries restricts the clothing women may wear, the jobs they may do and their rights to marry and divorce. The law in some of these countries even prescribes 'wifely obedience'. The social, cultural and religious practices of several countries dictate that young girls are subject to genital mutilation and forced child marriages.

GENDER AT WORK

- The number of women participating in the labour force has stagnated – decreasing from fifty-seven percent in 1990 to fifty-five percent in 2013.
- On average, women earn ten to thirty percent less than working men.
- Women are only half as likely as men to have full-time waged jobs for an employer.
- In only 5 of the 114 countries for which data are available (Colombia, Fiji, Jamaica, Lesotho and the Philippines) have women reached parity with men in occupations such as legislators, senior officials and managers.
- Women spend at least twice as much time as men on unpaid domestic work, such as caring and housework.
- 128 countries have at least one sex-based legal differentiation, meaning women and men cannot function in the world of work in the same way as men; in 54 countries, women face 5 or more legal differences.
- In developing countries, there is a nine percentage-point gap between the number of women and men who have an account at a formal financial institution.
- More than one in three women has experienced either physical or sexual violence by a partner or non-partner sexual violence.
- In 2010–12, forty-two countries reported sex differentials of more than ten percent in secondary school enrolment rates.
- One in three girls in developing countries is married before she reaches her 18th birthday.

In Saudi Arabia, for example, women are not permitted to drive cars. Under Sharia law (for instance, as in Saudi Arabia) a woman's evidence in court is worth half that of a man. Justice is clearly not served when sex discrimination of this kind is either permitted or legally decreed. But several theories of justice reduce or altogether exclude women from consideration. Feminist theorists have sought to expose this deficiency.

Feminism

Feminism is far from being a one-dimensional theory. We need to differentiate, however briefly, the major strands within feminist theory, but I shall discuss only the three most prominent groups: liberal, radical and difference feminists.

The struggle against the oppression of women has a long history. In 1792, Mary Wollstonecraft's (1759–1797) *A Vindication of the Rights of Women* was based on the (now unsurprising) premise that women are rational creatures and therefore have the ability to exercise civil duties, even though at that time in Britain they were deprived of complete political rights. The inheritors of this approach are *liberal feminists*, who embrace individual rights, both civil and political. Liberal feminists regard all people as autonomous, rights-bearing agents and they stress the values of equality, rationality and autonomy. Liberal feminism's dominant claim is that equality of reason between the sexes ought to secure equality of opportunity to effect rational choices. Liberal feminists generally recognize that society tends, in many respects, to be male-dominated but, unlike radical feminists, they do not launch a comprehensive assault on this domination in the social, political and economic sphere. Instead, they prefer to work to change the ways in which society discriminates against women, particularly in the arena of employment. In simple terms, liberal feminism emphasizes *equality,* while radical feminism, as we shall see, concentrates on *difference.*

Liberal feminists have conducted legal and political campaigns, for example to criminalize violence against women. They have also demonstrated how the distinction between the private and public spheres has fostered male domination of women by treating domestic power relations as 'normal' and therefore beyond the reach of the law. Similarly, they have exposed how the traditional concept of the household and the role of women as childbearers has concealed male domination of women in the home from public awareness, even overlooking spousal rape, which, although an offence in many countries, is not regarded as a crime in several others, including India, Bangladesh, Sri Lanka, Burma, Singapore, Ethiopia and Finland.

Radical feminists (who include those who advocate socialist and Marxist feminism) challenge the way in which society is arranged, in particular, the power that men exercise over women socially, politically and economically. They oppose the notion of conventional sex roles. Radical feminists generally seek to eliminate patriarchy by attacking existing institutions and values rather than through the political process. The focus of radical feminists is on the differences they identify between the sexes. Men, they argue, define women as different so as to dominate them; the issue is fundamentally one of power. And these differences are often 'sexualized'. For example, men are regarded as rational, women as irrational; men are active, women passive; men are objective, women subjective. The world is man-made; it licenses the subjugation of and violence against women. Some radical feminists doubt the ability of the law to produce genuine equality. They raise what is called the 'woman question', which seeks to expose the gender implications of laws and practices that appear to be neutral or objective. As the leading radical feminist Catharine MacKinnon (1946–) puts it, 'Abstract rights … authorise the male experience of the world'.

She argues that the concept of 'rights' is formal, hierarchical and patriarchal and that the law in general reflects and defends a male viewpoint. For example, the First Amendment of the United States constitution protects freedom of expression. But, she claims, it is one of several 'abstract rights' that protect the right to pornography and, in effect, allow men to degrade and exploit women.

The individualism advocated by liberal feminists is derided by many of its radical detractors as insufficient, because it fails to recognize the problems that lie in the distribution of individual rights. Radical feminists seek to eliminate male social and economic domination by a fundamental restructuring of society rather than by the exclusively political process pursued by liberal feminists.

Another group of feminists, the so-called *difference feminists*, analyze the differences between the sexes, for example, that women are instinctively more nurturing than men. Some difference feminists concentrate on the differences between men and women that are *socially* created ('social difference feminism'), while others examine the *symbolic and psychological* influences on these differences ('symbolic difference feminism'). Difference feminism rejects the way in which liberal feminists embrace the notion of formal equality, arguing that it undercuts the differences between the sexes.

Difference feminists focus on the *positive* differences between the sexes, such as the 'special bond' women form with other women. This contrasts with radical feminists, who concentrate on the *negative* differences, such as the sexual objectification of women. Difference feminists also concentrate on the positive features of women's identity and how they should be cherished and valued. In the words of the Belgian philosopher, linguist and psychoanalyst Luce Irigary (1930–), 'the pretext of the neutral individual does not pass the reality test: women get pregnant, not men; women and little girls are raped, boys very rarely; the bodies of women and girls are used for involuntary prostitution and pornography, those of men infinitely less'.

The key point of difference feminism is that the concept of equality is a more complex and inexact than liberals would suggest. In her influential text, *In a Different Voice: Psychological Theory and Women's Development*, Carol Gilligan (1936–) attempts to show that women's moral values tend to accentuate *responsibility*, whereas men's emphasize *rights*. She describes the male 'voice' as 'logical and individualistic', by which she means that men stress the protection of individual rights and justice. The feminine voice, on the other hand, places more emphasis on the protection of interpersonal relationships and caring for others. She argues that androgyny – assimilating the masculine and the feminine – is the ideal way to fulfil one's human potential. Her analysis of the female 'care perspective' has important implications for what we as a society regard as just. She argues that we need to adopt an approach that recognizes the fundamental differences between men and women. Her theory has been criticized as both speculative, since the data on which she relies is rather limited and 'anti-male'.

Feminism and theories of justice

The main target of many feminist writers is the social contract, especially as presented by John Rawls. In the words of Susan Moller Okin (1946–2004), the social contract manifests 'blindness to sexism'. Okin points to Rawls's concept of, 'people in the original position', which, though she calls it 'brilliant', overlooks the importance of the family. She argues that one of the central planks of liberalism – the sanctity of the private sphere – ignores what goes on in society inside the home and conceals the deep inequalities that spring from women's child-bearing duties. These significantly reduce their opportunities to compete in the so-called free market which, as Okin shows, shrinks their earning power.

Although Rawls specifies that the family is a major social institution, he fails to extend his principles of justice to it. Why, Okin asks, does he consider the manner in which families distribute fundamental rights and duties to be outside his concept of justice, especially when one considers their social, economic and political ramifications? Rawls acknowledges the family as an important part of the basic structure of society, with the potential powerfully to affect the opportunities of its members, especially women. In one essay he likens the family to other associations, such as churches, universities, companies and trade unions that cannot violate the basic rights and freedoms of the equal citizens who are its members. But, he implies, like them, the family is not itself subject to the principles of justice. We don't expect churches, he says, to be democratically governed; similarly we should not require families to be governed by the principles of justice.

The boundary between public and private is a pivotal principle of liberal theory that has implications for our understanding of what constitutes a just society. Legal intrusion into the private domain has long concerned liberals, who have generally sought to keep the law's long arm out of the home. But radical feminists, among others, argue that there is a serious downside to this approach as it can prevent effective criminal investigation and prosecution of domestic violence and allow the routine abuse of women in the private domain. You can see how delicate the challenge is that feminists face in pursuit of sexual justice. Happily, over the years, feminist theory has been able to confront and surmount several forms of sexual discrimination that have proved more intractable in non-liberal, undemocratic societies.

Concern about the social contract extends beyond Rawls to the works of earlier advocates, especially Hobbes and Locke (discussed in Chapter 5). At first blush, Hobbes appears to be sympathetic to the rights of women. Indeed, he maintains that the idea of equality derives, in part, from the fact that we are all naturally vulnerable to domination and capable of dominating others. And since women are naturally free, if they fall under another's power, their agreement is required, and so they are included in his social contract. He is clear in his repudiation of patriarchy and claims sovereigns may be male or female. But in spite of his apparently enlightened view, Pateman, in *The Sexual Contract*, shows how Hobbes's idea of an absolute political sovereign to maintain the peace is mirrored in another concept he advocates, that of the despotic head of a family, even though he concedes that a woman could be in command. In describing a family as 'the father … the children and the slaves united in one civil person by virtue of paternal power' he completely omits to mention the wife or mother!

Hobbes's concept of the commonwealth draws a parallel between paternal and sovereign power, He claims that fathers form societies, not mothers. Pateman is no less critical of Locke. While Locke describes the nuclear family as a social unit that paves the way towards political society, he relegates women to the menial role of procreation and obedience to their husbands. It is hard to find evidence of his vaunted 'natural rights' being accorded to women. Describing the family as a 'voluntary compact' (that is, a contract) between a man and a woman, he defines its chief purpose as procreation and providing for the ensuing progeny. But he recognizes certain limits on the husband's power, for example, the right of a woman to leave her husband. Difference feminists, such as Iris Marion Young (1949–2006), look beyond distributive justice to the removal of what she describes as the institutionalized control and subjugation of women. It is, she argues, a result of the injustices of the 'often unconscious assumptions and reactions of well-meaning people in ordinary interactions, media and cultural stereotypes and structural features of bureaucratic hierarchies and market mechanisms – in short, the normal processes of everyday life'. She identifies five 'faces of oppression': exploitation, marginalization, powerlessness, cultural imperialism and violence.

The extent to which women are objectified, usually sexually, is an important theme in the feminist critique of theories of justice. Treating a woman as an object, they point out, includes denying her agency, autonomy and the capacity to speak. Feminist critique of theories of justice generally focus on the abstract nature of social contractarianism, which fails to account for the everyday inequalities and mistreatment endured by women. MacKinnon and Andrea Dworkin (1946–2005) extend Kant's argument that extra-marital sex and prostitution reduce women to objects to society at large, arguing that women are objectified by men in general. This condition is shaped by pornography which, MacKinnon claims, depicts women as sex objects available for male consumption: 'A person, in one Kantian view, is a free and rational agent whose existence is an end in itself, as opposed to instrumental. In pornography women exist to the *end* of male pleasure'. The availability of pornography breeds inequality. The problem is not, as Kant maintains, sexuality, but the way sexuality is presented by pornographic images, and it may lead to real violence against women.

Unlike Kant, Dworkin and MacKinnon are sceptical about his argument that sex within marriage is an equal and reciprocal arrangement. They recognize the objectification of women as a factor in *all* heterosexual relationships, in part owing to the cultural and social sources of sexist norms quite apart from pornography: the media, music, literature and family.

Disability

You will recall that the participants in Rawls's original position are stripped of their identity. They vote in a hypothetical bubble for the terms of the contract that offers the greatest prospect of justice for their community. The veil of ignorance, however, does not extend to their being concealed from disability, because Rawls stipulates that the contract-makers would be 'fully co-operating' during their lives. There is therefore no reason why they should believe that, when the veil is lifted, they will turn out to be disabled. The marginalization of people with physical or mental impairments (for example, in respect of employment, access, transport, housing and so on) poses a serious problem for the achievement of justice and equality and a challenge to theories of justice that purport to apply to all. Nussbaum protests at this general silence:

> What have theories of justice in the social contract tradition said about these problems? Virtually nothing. Nor can the omission be easily corrected, for it is built into the structure of our strongest theories.

It is possible to take a less rigid view of Rawls's original position. One could argue that there is nothing that *explicitly* excludes the physically or mentally impaired. In 2001, Rawls did adjust his account of the original position to acknowledge that the participants represent people in a future society rather than those in that society denied knowledge of their social position. If they recognize the prospect that those who they represent might turn out to be disabled, they may speak up for their welfare. But this would seem to demand an imagination beyond the reach of most ordinary individuals.

Such modifications dilute the contractual essence of the model. Where else could we look for a satisfactory theory that meets the needs of the disabled? One possibility, briefly canvassed in Chapter 9, is the idea of 'luck egalitarianism' advanced by, among others, Ronald Dworkin. It claims that injustices are a failure in the distribution of 'brute luck' – a benefit or detriment that is not my fault. The opposite is 'option luck', where I take a deliberate risk. For Dworkin any inequality caused by option luck creates no claims of justice. It is therefore only those disabilities consequential upon bad brute luck that generate justice claims.

When I choose to gamble with my money or my health, I can hardly complain that I have suffered unjustly. For some theorists, this takes the notion of individual responsibility too far. It has been argued, for example, that a disabled person's bad luck lies not so much in their physical or mental impairment as in having to cope in an environment that lacks proper facilities such as wheelchair access.

What's fair?

In the case of the disabled, how do we measure what counts as a just distribution of social goods? Social contractarians, in pursuit of objectivity, generally look to individuals' rights and opportunities. Thus wealth is taken by Rawls to be one of the 'social primary goods'. When applied to the disabled, however, this measurement overlooks the conditions under which these goods are used: if I am confined to a wheelchair, my opportunities to enjoy my wealth or income are altered. This may suggest that, as we discussed in Chapter 7, the acquisition of rights is one thing, their actualization another. The advocates of the capabilities approach advance an alternative based on the tangible needs of the disabled and the creation of a compassionate environment that facilitates their human flourishing. Applying Nussbaum's inventory of basic capabilities to the disabled requires the provision of physical modifications to buildings, suitable vehicles, vehicular access and so on. Moreover, it advances disabled people's capacity to flourish as individuals by treating them with respect. Other writers propose less far-reaching measures, including financial compensation, medical procedures or technological aids to improve people's prospects of obtaining greater equality. There is, however, always the risk of antagonizing disabled people by patronizing or according superficially equal treatment that neglects their deeper human needs, particularly their relationships.

What about fair distribution? How can a society both accord equal respect to the disabled and remedy their major problems? Redistribution may actually be counter-productive; it could increase the shame and embarrassment of disabled people by underscoring the perception that they are inadequate members of society. Some argue that to ascribe a person's incapacity to innate attributes is to treat an individual as somehow inferior and thus less than able to contribute to the welfare of the community. It would be better, they say, to defend any remedial initiatives on the grounds that it rectifies unfair discrimination against disabled people. Others respond that there is no suggestion of inferiority, merely recognition that certain human abilities are more important than others and that disability is a matter of degree rather than type. Many of us have certain physical or mental weaknesses but we are not necessarily perceived as inferior. Improving the plight of those whose disabilities are severe is best achieved by devoting more resources to them.

Problems of identity

It is self-evidently wrong to treat all disabled people as belonging to a single group. Not only are some impairments more apparent than others, but we are all individuals with our own identity and concept of our place in the world. Some people adjust better to their disabilities than others. It is also important to observe that being labelled 'disabled' may result in discrimination of various kinds. Those of us who are fortunate enough to be able-bodied may lack an understanding of the privations and distress suffered by disabled people.

I recently experienced a temporary and trivial example of a disability that afflicts millions. I had an irritating pain in my left ear. My doctor examined both canals and pronounced a single word: 'wax!' He prescribed some drops, which he promised would soften the egregious substance. This would, he said, render the syringing he recommended I undergo a week later 'less painful'. I duly administered the drops and was rendered instantly and almost completely deaf, enveloped in a prison of alarming silence. I realized that I had never taken deafness seriously. But deafness is no joke. As a music lover, I was bereft. Even typing without the reassuring click of keyboard and mouse was disconcerting. I instinctively avoided contact with others. The perils and frustrations of even the most normal, quotidian tasks were countless. Crossing the road was transformed into a soundless nightmare. I couldn't risk driving. The usual domestic noises, doorbell, telephone, radio, vanished.

My very brief exposure to hearing loss ended after a week but it was a chastening experience. Technology can and does help the deaf. Advanced hearing aids and other devices must be of considerable benefit to those living with this disability. Cochlear implants hold out hope, although they are still expensive and reportedly not always effective. Subtitles and signing assist greatly. Yet this is a dreadful disability. There are some seventy million deaf people in the world. In Britain alone eleven million people – one in six of the population – endure some form of deafness. Within twenty years there are likely to be nearly sixteen million. Almost a million are severely deaf. Some 50,000 children cannot hear. Sign language is the main form of communication for 24,000 people. As people approach the age of seventy, the prospects of suffering deafness of various degrees are alarming: seventy percent will succumb. I am ashamed to confess that it took a temporary loss of this vital sense to knock some common sense into me. I discovered the existence of 'deaf culture': a set of values that extends to beliefs, literary traditions, art, history and common associations of communities affected by deafness whose members employ sign language as their principal mode of communicating. It is interesting to note that its members generally reject the idea that deafness is a disability, preferring to regard it as a different form of human experience.

A number of feminist philosophers also lament the inadequacy of traditional accounts of justice in their treatment of disability. In particular, they point to the difficulties many disabled women face in respect of their access to fertility treatment and custody of their children. More broadly, feminist disability theory explores the extent to which physical or cognitive impairment encumbers women's social, economic and political prospects. The natural physical fragility of women has long resulted in their being treated as outsiders because of their failure to conform to social or biological archetypes. Feminist theory understandably discounts this element as a source of sex-related differences and looks instead to societal factors that may account for mental or cognitive disparities. There is, however, a tendency to connect the perspectives of disabled individuals to biological factors, thereby explaining intellectual outlook by reference to physical determinants.

You can see why the capabilities approach, with its emphasis on compassion, care and respect for human dignity, has considerable purchase when it comes to the predicament of disabled people. Rawlsian social contractarianism and the ethical foundations of Kantian and Humean liberalism present an incomplete model of human co-operation that favours the able-bodied.

Animals

Do we have any moral responsibility towards non-human creatures? If they are merely expendable objects, then the answer is probably no. If, on the other hand, animals deserve our concern and respect as fellow inhabitants of the planet, then we have a duty to justify morally the suffering we inflict on these sentient beings. The suffering that is caused by subjecting animals to a variety of cruel practices imposes a moral obligation to discontinue those practices or, at least, to reduce their pain. This includes ending or regulating vivisection, hunting, battery farming, trapping, rodeos, circuses, bull-fighting, some zoos, the fur trade, the conditions under which animals are transported to the slaughterhouse and the manner in which their lives are terminated.

What about justice? Only humans participate in Rawls's experiment. Animals cannot, of course, be expected to debate the principles of justice, but they belong to our world. Indeed, they have been here much longer. Rawls does concede, in *A Theory of Justice,* that since they are sentient, animals are owed moral duties:

> Certainly it is wrong to be cruel to animals and the destruction of a whole species can be a great evil. The capacity for feelings of pleasure and pain and for the forms of life of which animals are capable clearly impose duties of compassion and humanity in their case … They are outside the scope of the theory of justice and it does not seem possible to extend the contract so as to include them in a natural way.

Animals, he claims, lack those properties by virtue of which they are to be treated in accordance with the principles of justice. What are these properties? First is a capacity for a conception of the good and for a sense of justice. Second is the power to be a fully co-operating member of society. Only humans possess these. Robert Nozick (whose libertarian entitlement theory we considered in Chapter 6) asks whether we have a right to sacrifice animals for human pleasure. Suppose snapping your fingers to music increases your happiness. Yet what if you knew that by the same snap you could cause 10,000 contented cows to die, either in great pain and suffering or painlessly. Would it be morally wrong to snap? Or suppose that you enjoy swinging a baseball bat but a cow's head happens to be in the path of your bat and you smash its skull? Is this any different from hunting for pleasure? What if you hired someone to do the killing for you?

If eating meat is not necessary for health and only gives pleasure, can we justify killing animals to maximize that pleasure? Is there a moral distinction between killing a cow to eat it for pleasure and killing it to enjoy the pleasure of swinging a baseball bat? Nozick argues against regarding individual rights as an end; we ought instead to perceive rights negatively, as what he calls 'side constraints' on our conduct. He stops short of supporting the view that animals possess equal moral status to people; it is part of his larger argument against utilitarian justifications for liberalism.

Their moral status

What do the great philosophers have to say? Aristotle distinguishes animals from humans on the grounds that while humans have *logos* (reason or language), animals are *aloga* (without *logos*). Descartes (1596–1650) views animals as mere biological instruments, without any subjective awareness. Locke, however, argues that animals have feelings and that preventable cruelty is morally wrong; the right not to be harmed vests in the owner of the animal or in the person who is being impaired by such cruelty. St Thomas Aquinas and Immanuel Kant both reject the idea that humans have direct duties toward non-human animals.

Today the question of justice toward animals has spawned substantial debate and a huge literature. At its core is the degree to which animals ought to be protected by recognizing that they have rights, if not by according them rights, then through some other means to protect their welfare. Those who support animal rights generally argue that because animals are sentient creatures and hence enjoy a subjective good, they have moral status and deserve certain rights, especially the right to life and the right not to be exploited for human benefit. On the other hand, it is argued that sentience is inadequate to be a bearer of rights; there is an additional requirement of cognitive ability, such as rationality or the capacity to reason morally. As only humans appear to have this facility, we are at liberty to exploit those who do not. Those who support animal rights respond that it is arbitrary to restrict rights to those who enjoy cognitive capacity.

Kant claims that animals belong to the deterministic dominion of nature. Only humans surmount this realm because we are capable of moral rationality. Animals, unlike us, may be used as means to an end. Human dignity and moral capacity are fundamentally distinct from the natural world. Only humans possess dignity; only humans belong in the realm of ends. It is on this ground that he concludes that we have no moral duties to animals. They have only a relative value in respect of our ends. Cruelty to animals is wrong, Kant asserts, only because of its negative effects on humans. He offers this example. If a man shoots his faithful old dog because the animal is no longer capable of service, he does not fail in his duty to the dog, for the dog cannot judge, but his act is inhuman and damages the humanity which it is his duty to show towards all mankind. If he is not to stifle his human feelings, he must practise kindness towards animals, for he who is cruel to animals also becomes hard in his dealings with men.

Rawls, as mentioned, explicitly excludes animals as rational agents. But I cannot see any reason why, even though they are not asked to imagine themselves as members of another species, the people in the original position, behind their veil of ignorance, would not select a moral system that included respect for animals. At most, Rawls's social contract could require *indirect* duties towards animals because of the contingent features of the social contract agreed in any particular society or out of respect for human sensibilities in regard to animals. This does not, however, seem a solid basis on which to build a compassionate approach towards non-humans. A more promising form of contractarianism is proposed by Thomas Scanlon (1940–), who suggests that by using the concept of trustees, acting on behalf of the animals, the people in the original position could be asked to accept certain principles that support the interests of non-humans.

A utilitarian standpoint would appear to offer greater promise. The pain of a few may in principle be justified by the pleasure of (or at least the benefits to) the many. Utilitarian hostility to killing a conscious being is based on the destruction of potential future pleasures. Killing a creature is wrong not because it harms the animal killed, but because its death diminishes the sum of the utilitarian calculus. Peter Singer (1946–), in his seminal book *Animal Liberation*, adopts an act-utilitarian position whose principal claim is that, in calculating the consequences of our actions, the pain suffered or pleasure enjoyed by animals should count no less than our own, to assert otherwise constitutes 'speciesism'. Animals have moral worth; their lives are not simply dispensable, nor ought they be exploited for our own ends. He does not maintain that the lives of humans and animals have *equal* worth or that they call for equal treatment, except in respect of the capacity to experience pleasure and pain. Animals do not need to be *treated* equally but they are entitled to equal *consideration*.

Vivisection, Singer argues, is therefore justifiable, provided suffering is limited to a minimum and the research is highly likely to produce aggregate benefits outweighing individual pain. His test is whether it would be morally acceptable to perform a particular experiment on mentally retarded human orphans (to exclude the possibility of vicarious suffering of relatives). If not, it is speciesist to inflict pain on animals of similar intelligence. Laboratory experiments, often painful, on live animals are sometimes justified by the claim that science is somehow value-neutral. This is a convenient expedient to blind scientists to the distress of animals and deny animals' subjective awareness and moral status. The strength of the utilitarian argument lies in its emphasis on actual *suffering*, which is in line with our instinctive

COMPASSION TOWARDS ANIMALS

Albert Schweitzer (French-German theologian, 1875–1965): 'We must fight against the spirit of unconscious cruelty with which we treat the animals. Animals suffer as much as we do. True humanity does not allow us to impose such sufferings on them. It is our duty to make the whole world recognize it. Until we extend our circle of compassion to all living things, humanity will not find peace.'

Leonardo da Vinci (Italian polymath, 1452–1519): 'I have from an early age abjured the use of meat and the time will come when men such as I will look upon the murder of animals as they now look upon the murder of men.'

Bernard E. Rollin (American philosopher, 1943–): '[A]nimals have been allowed to suffer in research not through cruelty but rather, because consideration of suffering is forgotten in the thrill of the pursuit, by nature ultimately ruthless, complemented by an ideology which discounts the cogency of moral reflection in scientific activity and denies the meaningfulness of attributing feelings to animals and is coupled with practical pressures.'

Stephen R.L. Clark (British philosopher, 1945–): 'It is in the name of science, and with the specious bribe of release from all our ills, that we have been cajoled and threatened and insulted into permitting the continued torture of our kindred and the continued blunting of the sensibilities of those who come to work in our laboratories. Let no one rely on common decency in such a situation: the pressure of one's professional peer-group, the atmosphere of dismissive tolerance of all outside the clan, the calm assumption that this is what we do, are all far too strong for most of us to resist.'

feelings about animals and pronounced by Bentham in his remark that the question to ask about animals '… is not Can they reason? nor Can they talk? but, Can they suffer?' Its weakness resides in its neglect of *individual* animals and its inclination to accept the use of animals where likely benefits outweigh the costs of suffering.

As discussed above and in Chapter 7, the capabilities approach presents a viable alternative to both utilitarian and Rawlsian conceptions of justice. Nussbaum applies its central ideas to animals so that 'no sentient animal should be cut off from the chance of a flourishing life, a life with the type of dignity relevant to that species and that all sentient animals should enjoy certain positive opportunities to flourish'. Unlike contractarianism, it endorses *direct* obligations of justice to animals; these duties do not derive from those we owe to humans. And it accepts that animals are subjects with an entitlement to flourish and who are therefore subjects of justice *in their own right*, not merely objects of compassion. Unlike utilitarianism, it respects each individual creature, declining to aggregate the good of different lives and forms of lives. Animals are not to be used as a means to the ends of others or of society as a whole.

But for an animal to thrive, different considerations apply. In the case of humans, the capabilities approach does not seek to draw norms directly from facts about human nature. We evaluate, says Nussbaum, the innate powers of human beings, enquiring which are good and which are central to a decently flourishing human life, a life with dignity. An *ethical* appraisal is therefore primary. Her list of capabilities in respect of humans (summarized in Chapter 7) plainly requires some adaptation in the case of animals. For example, her first requirement, 'life' and its continuation, is extended to all animals, regardless of whether they have such a conscious interest. All sentient animals have an entitlement against gratuitous killing for sport or for luxury items such as fur. In the case of food, the approach seems unclear: animals may be killed painlessly following a healthy and free-ranging life but what of the termination of the lives of very young animals? The second requirement, bodily health, requires the legal prohibition of cruelty and neglect. In regard to the capability of 'emotions', it is obvious that sentient creatures experience a range of feelings, including fear, anger, gratitude, grief and pleasure. Some animals, ethologists have shown, demonstrate compassion. They are, like us, entitled to lives that enable them to have attachments and to love and care for others.

Some go further and argue that animals should be vested with *rights*. But the idea that an animal is able to be a right-holder is anathema to many theorists. How can an agent who is incapable of exercising *duties* be capable of exercising rights? We should, however, distinguish between a legal and a moral right. Legal rights include legislation against animal cruelty, which may be construed as conferring on animals a legal right to be treated humanely. Moral right includes an entitlement to do certain things and the moral restraint on others to refrain from interference. Animals' enjoyment of moral rights would seem to offer a more promising argument, especially if the 'interest' theory of rights is adopted. This approach is widely accepted in the case of children whose rights are exercised by their parents or guardians. The child has no choice in the matter, yet we do not say that children have no rights. A similar point could be made in relation to animals.

It is generally thought that since chimpanzees are incapable of responsibilities and cannot be held legally accountable for their actions, they cannot be endowed with legal rights, including the right to freedom. Contrast this with the judgement of an Indian court in the *Nair* v *Union of India case in 2000*:

> [W]e hold that circus animals ... are housed in cramped cages, subjected to fear, hunger, pain, not to mention the undignified way of life they have to live, with no respite and the impugned notification has been issued in conformity with ... the values of human life, philosophy of the Constitution ... Though not homosapiens, [*sic*] they are also beings entitled to dignified existence and humane treatment sans cruelty and torture ... Therefore it is our fundamental duty to show compassion to our animal friends but also to recognise and protect their rights ... If humans are entitled to fundamental rights, why not animals?

Yet another perspective in support of animals is 'sentimental anthropomorphicism'. This is advanced by the philosopher Tom Regan (1938–), who argues for the similarities between a human and an animal life. In particular, animals, like humans, are 'subjects-of-a-life'. They have inherent, not merely instrumental, value or worth. This entitles them to the absolute right to live their lives with respect and autonomy. As he says in his book, *The Case for Animal Rights*:

> The most reasonable criterion of right-possession … is not that of sentience or having interests, since neither of these by themselves can account for why it is wrong to treat humans who are not irreversibly comatose merely as means; rather the criterion that most adequately accounts for this is the criterion of inherent value: All those beings (and only those beings) which have inherent value have rights.

Benefit to humans, however great, justifies the violation of this absolute right. But, as you will have deduced, not only do some (including theorists sympathetic to the animal cause) consider the attribution of rights a step too far, but communitarians denounce rights as excessively individualist. Moreover, they are perceived to operate formally, without necessarily assisting those (the poor or oppressed) who most need them, or they are dismissed as 'excess baggage,' redundant in the disapproval of cruelty or abuse. Does Regan's argument that animals have an inherent value lead inexorably to a rights-based conclusion? Even if it does, the language of rights does not seem a very practicable or realistic foundation for the protection of animals against needless suffering. It may be that justice requires a change in our social and economic systems to secure a sustainable future for our planet and its inhabitants.

You may think that concern for justice to animals is misdirected. Shouldn't the elimination of human suffering occupy us far more than the plight of other creatures? It is sometimes said that people involved in animal rights or animal welfare either subordinate human interests to animal interests or have a pathological indifference towards human beings. This has not been my experience; those dedicated to the animal welfare movement are often also committed to the alleviation of suffering of oppressed or disadvantaged humans. For example, there was a long association between the feminist and the anti-vivisection campaigns in nineteenth-century Britain. Contemporary feminist theorists discern a relationship between the treatment of women and animals. As MacKinnon puts it:

> Women have been animalized, animals feminized, often at the same time. If qualified entrance into the human race on male terms has little for women – granted, we are not eaten but then that is not our inequality problem – how much will being seen as humanlike but not fully so, do for other animals?

Is our concern for animals connected to our general apprehensions about the depredations we visit on our environment and the consequences of this damage to all living things? Animal cruelty and indifference to the loss of endangered species are occasionally defended in the name of cultural or ethical relativism. This entails the claim that there is a complex variety among cultures; each culture is distinctive, with its parts so entwined that none can be understood or appraised without reference to other parts. The doctrine implies 'ethical relativism', which asserts that the moral rightness and wrongness of actions differs from society to society; there are no universal enduring, moral absolutes. It is a precarious belief that may be defeated either by refuting the claim that morality is at all contingent on social factors or by contesting the view that a diversity of cultures, and hence moral principles, has always existed. Plato supported the first – absolutist – view, maintaining that the strength of moral values is logically independent of social or cultural background; ethics is as scientific a pursuit as mathematics. Adopting this view risks the stigma of ethnocentricity but it is hard to see how, if, say, torturing an infant is wrong in London, it is not also wrong in Lahore.

We turn a blind eye to the suffering inflicted on creatures whose pain is visible and palpable. Take the example of bear farming in China and Vietnam. The plight of thousands of endangered Asiatic black bears makes horrifying reading. After being trapped in the wild, they are confined in tiny wire cages no bigger than their bodies. Metal catheters up to seven inches long are inserted into their abdomens to 'milk' them of their bile, which is used in Oriental medicines and preparations. Many spend their entire lives (which may last up to twenty years) subject to this torture. In the minds of some otherwise intelligent people this appalling practice is defended on the ground that these creatures are mere objects, therefore the question of their well-being, let alone whether they can be said to have rights, simply does not arise. But, as the philosopher Schopenhauer (1788–1860) declares: 'The assumption that animals are without rights and the illusion that our treatment of them has no moral significance is a positively outrageous example of Western crudity and barbarity. Universal compassion is the only guarantee of morality'.

If justice towards animals is ultimately treated as a part of our concern for the earth and its entire flora and fauna, we need to understand the conditions that cause pain to animals. Once comprehended, it is arguable that to end the misery we inflict on animals is not merely a matter of moral duty but one of social justice.

Summing up

This chapter has identified three groups that tend to be neglected by leading theories of justice: women, the disabled and animals.

While discrimination against women has decreased, thanks to reforms in domestic and international law and increased social and cultural recognition of the injustice of this inequality, the treatment of women and girls in many non-western countries continues to be a major source of concern. Feminists of various affiliations have played, and still play, a crucial role in extinguishing the numerous inequities that persist in a male-dominated world.

Disabled people encounter discrimination, both direct and indirect, in the workplace, housing, health care, education and transport. They often experience difficulties gaining access to shops, banks, cafés and other places. The law of many countries, as well as international instruments, recognizes the rights of disabled people to equal treatment. The United Nations Convention on Disability Rights has been signed by some 140 nations. It establishes a recognized international standard to be adopted in respect of the rights of disabled people and requires signatories to report regularly to the UN on the steps they have taken to protect and promote the rights of people with disabilities.

There is a growing acceptance in many societies of the injustice caused by cruelty inflicted on non-human animals. There are a wide variety of approaches to this matter, including the legal recognition of animal rights on the grounds that animals are entitled to the possession of their own lives and that their basic interests – such as the avoidance of suffering – ought to receive the same consideration as is given to human beings. The chapter canvassed several other theories, including the deontological perspective that claims that some creatures are 'subjects of a life', with a sense of their own future, who ought to be treated as ends in themselves, not as means to an end. Utilitarians, however, emphasize the interests, rather than rights, that animals have, particularly the interest in avoiding suffering. They argue that animals may legitimately be eaten or used in other ways, provided there is no unnecessary suffering. Some critics contend that since animals cannot perform duties they cannot possess rights. Numerous animal rights and welfare groups continue to campaign for compassion in the treatment of animals and for stricter legal and regulatory standards that prevent or avoid cruelty, pain and suffering.

11 Communitarianism

We are all part of a community. We belong to a place – a city, a suburb or a village – that we call 'home'. It may be the place where we were born, where we grew up or where we now live. But there are also what have been called 'communities of memory' which share a history that members seek to re-invigorate in pursuit of the common good; these include one's nation or a particular language-based group. In addition there are the communities of which we are a part as a result of shared activity or experience: family, school, university, workplace and so on.

Communitarians support principles that enhance the interests of the community, civic virtue and social solidarity. The core of justice, they claim, is to be found in the answer to the question of what constitutes a good life. The leading communitarian, Michael Sandel (1953–), shows how we generally have a sense of 'solidarity' towards institutions such as our family, country and religion that does not arise from any contract. Communitarians emphasize the development and improvement of character, decency, individual responsibility and virtues in the public domain. Communitarianism seeks to enhance these values through education, community-based groups, the family and civil society. It is presented as a positive approach to questions of public policy. Although it acknowledges human self-interest, it believes in the possibility of creating a better society founded on co-operation in pursuit of constructive community goals.

As an example, Sandel asks you to imagine that you see two children drowning. You have time to save only one. One child is yours. Which do you save? Is it wrong to rescue your own child? Would it be better to toss a coin? Most of us would accept that saving your own child is perfectly acceptable. It is a matter of our moral duty towards members of our own family. This notion of membership or belonging is well captured by Alasdair MacIntyre in his book *After Virtue*:

> We all approach our own circumstances as bearers of a particular social identity. I am someone's son or daughter, someone's cousin or uncle; a citizen of this or that city … I belong to this clan, that tribe, this nation. Hence what is good for me has to be the good for someone who inhabits these roles. As such, I inherit from the past of my family, my city, my tribe, my nation a variety of debts, inheritances, expectations and obligations. These constitute the given of my life, my moral starting point. This is, in part, what gives my life its moral particularity.

This is very different from the Kantian view (discussed in Chapter 3) in which what is right takes precedence over what is good. That is to say priority is given to claims based on the rights of individuals over claims based on the good that would result to them, or to others, from violating those rights. Communitarians reject this view and claim that it is unacceptable to abstract justice in this way and that standards of justice are inseparable from the practice, beliefs and traditions of particular societies.

Kant, on the other hand, argues that what is 'right' trumps other values that are contingent on want-satisfaction because they arise from the concept of freedom that is a precondition of all human ends. In other words, the principles of justice that define our rights and duties should be *neutral*: they should be *silent* on the question of what constitutes a good life. To identify the moral law, both Kant and Rawls require people to disregard their objectives, attachments and concepts of the good. This is a far cry from Aristotle's view; he believes that principles of justice are not, nor should be, neutral about the good life, quite the opposite.

Other prominent communitarians – Alisdair MacIntyre (1929–), Charles Taylor (1931–) and Michael Walzer (1935–) – are united in their dismissal of Rawls's belief that the main function of government is to safeguard and distribute fairly the freedom and economic wealth that people need to live freely selected lives. They object to his assumption that his theory is universally valid, preferring a *contextual* approach that dictates that principles of justice be sought in the culture and traditions of specific communities. We need, argue Taylor and MacIntyre, to observe the world from the perspective of those who actually live in particular societies. They therefore reject the idea of an abstract, speculative hypothesis of what principles of justice imagined individuals behind a veil of ignorance might choose.

In his later work, *Political Liberalism*, Rawls strikes a slightly more sympathetic note towards communitarianism by diluting some of his earlier universalist assumptions. For example, he concedes that his theory is intended to apply only to societies in which people seek political consensus. In the *Law of Peoples*, he acknowledges that liberal democracy is not necessarily appropriate to all communities. In other words, a 'decent' society need not be democratic but it should be tolerant of other communities and domestically it ought to embrace a common concept of justice and protect basic human rights. Still, there is little doubt that he adheres to his model of a just society as presented in *A Theory of Justice*; it represents the ideal that sensible people would select and a prototype that warrants universal endorsement.

The communitarian view of justice, however, considers Rawls's individualism an inadequate account of what it is to be a person. The starting point of the communitarian view, presented influentially by Sandel, is that we are, in part, *defined* by our communities. We are social animals, rather than the egocentric, atomistic individuals conceived by Rawls. Moral obligation therefore springs from what the German philosopher Hegel (1770–1831) called the '*Sittlichkeit*' (moral life) of society. Communitarians reject the standpoint of duty-based liberalism in which we are perceived as transcendental, detached, independent and autonomous agents. None of us, they argue, can be properly understood as persons without reference to our social roles in the community as citizens, members of a family, a group or a nation. We are, as Sandel puts it, 'situated selves rather than unencumbered selves'.

Communitarians also spurn the individualism of human rights which, they claim, neglects community interests, civic virtue and social solidarity. The spirit of the communitarian standpoint lies in 'moral engagement' with our society, its morality and political life. This, in turn, requires us to reflect upon the nature and purpose of the good life. In Sandel's words, 'It may not be possible or even desirable, to deliberate about justice without deliberating about the good life'. This is, as I said, an unambiguous endorsement of the Aristotelean view of justice and a repudiation of the Kantian and Rawlsian approaches. It rejects the idea of an autonomous subject, preferring instead a world in which we are largely defined by our community that, in turn, is the source of our moral duties.

What's wrong with communitarianism?

This all sounds very reasonable and sensible. But communitarianism occasionally seems rather utopian, even though the source of the frustrations of communitarians is not hard to find. To them, liberalism appears to have been unable to address adequately the numerous problems of contemporary life: poverty, crime, loneliness, the breakdown of family life, selfishness, the avarice of the market, government bureaucracy, corruption and alienation from politics – to mention only a few. The fixation on individual rights in many societies reflects indifference towards the value of the participation in the public arena on which the flourishing of a genuine community depends. It can lead to egotism and selfishness and a preoccupation with one's own interests above those of one's community. Communitarians therefore advocate a stronger involvement in civic life. Instead of simply ignoring the moral and religious views of others, we should, they argue, challenge them, the better to learn and understand their standpoint and so arrive at a deeper sense of justice in society.

Communitarian theories do run into a few problems. In particular, they risk slipping into relativism. In his book, *Spheres of Justice*, the political theorist Michael Walzer argues we should 'look inside' particular societies and social groups to determine whether their practices are just, rather than relying on universal abstract principles. In addition, each 'sphere' of life generates its own norms of justice. Thus the norms that operate in the economic sphere differ from those in the educational. 'Justice', he declares, 'is relative to social meanings'. Is this a form of ethical or cultural relativism? If particular social norms and practices are defended in the name of community, where is the line to be drawn? Oppressive practices could easily be justified by reference to local culture. Respect for diversity in regard to religious and cultural values is all very well, but it is all too easy to allow this to become a smokescreen that conceals injustice. In our wish to comprehend sympathetically certain deplorable cultural or religious practices (for instance, female genital mutilation, 'honour' killings and the murder of homosexuals), we risk defending them.

Similarly, even if we can agree about the logic of certain moral precepts, their actual practical application is likely to differ substantially in societies that adhere to conflicting codes. For example, consensus on what could be considered an appropriate punishment for a crime will produce rather different results in a Western democracy than in a state governed by Islamic or Sharia law, whose penal code prescribes the amputation of a hand for the offence of theft.

FEMALE GENITAL MUTILATION

While the exact number is unknown, worldwide, at least two-hundred million girls between infancy and fifteen years old have been subjected to this non-medical procedure that has no health benefits. Of those two-hundred million girls, more than half live in just three countries – Indonesia, Egypt and Ethiopia.

FGM is most commonly practised in thirty countries across Africa, the Middle East and Asia and is defended on religious or cultural grounds. It involves the partial or total removal of external female genitalia and impedes the natural development and function of girls' and women's bodies. According to the UN World Health Organization, it can cause serious complications, both short-term and long-term, including severe pain and bleeding, infections, urinary problems, serious difficulties in childbirth, increased risk of death in newborn babies and the death of the victim herself.

FGM is internationally recognized as an infringement of the human rights of girls and women. It constitutes an extreme form of discrimination against women and, since it is almost always conducted on minors, it is also a violation of the rights of children.

The practice is increasingly being carried out in Western countries. In England, for example, the Health and Social Information Centre recently published, for the first time, details of the extent of the problem. It reported 5,700 newly-recorded cases of FGM during 2015–16. The vast majority of those procedures were carried out abroad, with only eighteen cases known to have been undertaken in the UK.

In December 2012, the UN General Assembly adopted a resolution on the elimination of female genital mutilation.

Little insight is required to distinguish the openness of democratic governments from the authoritarian administrations of many Asian societies. Conformity to Confucianism in China and other East Asian countries, notably Singapore, Malaysia and Indonesia, poses a major challenge to liberal democratic norms. Having lived in Hong Kong for many years, I am acutely aware of the rationale behind the arguments in support of so-called 'Asian values'. The communitarian foundations of Confucianism are evident in the significance the philosophy attaches to filial piety and devotion towards family, business and nation. In the words of Albert H.Y. Chen (1958–), the emphasis is on:

> the priority of the interests of the group, such as the family and the community … The individual is not an independent or self-sufficient entity but is always thought of as a member of a group and as dependent on the harmony and strength of the group

There is also an inclination by societies that cleave to Confucian values to sacrifice personal liberty in the interests of social stability and prosperity. Another important ethical ingredient is a strong emphasis on hard work and the pursuit of academic achievement, which was – fortunately – manifest in many of my Chinese students.

The concept of Asian values reached its zenith in the 1990s. In a quest for economic, ethical and social unity and a common identity, it promoted and celebrated the presence of shared norms across nation states in South-East and East Asia. Although these norms were, broadly speaking, hostile to individual liberty and democratic values, the 'miracle' of the spectacular success enjoyed by Asia's 'tiger economies' attracted international interest. Nevertheless, following the financial crisis of 1997, the doctrine began to lose traction when it became apparent that the region lacked a coherent policy or appropriate institutions to resolve the collapse of financial markets. The economic recovery – most conspicuously, of course, the rise of China as the world's second largest economy – has revived the debate about the significance of communitarian values and their challenge to the Western preoccupation with human rights and civil liberties. It has also engendered a reconsideration of some of the positive elements inherent in these values, such as the importance attached to education and the work ethic.

Communitarians rightly disdain the transferring of Western norms to regions that may be hostile to these values. It is fair to say that the recent attempts by the United States to export the western concept of democracy to countries in the Middle East and North Africa, such as Iraq and Afghanistan, have largely been unedifying and fruitless endeavours. Well-meaning though such efforts may be, transplanting western understandings and practices of democracy, liberalism and human rights to other countries has been a rather negative and ultimately futile undertaking. Walzer suggests that greater success might lie in abandoning abstract universalist ideas and instead pursuing a strategy of seeking to understand Asian values 'from within'. This entails adopting a more sensitive analysis of local justifications for the communitarian, Confucian resistance to individual rights, which is often centred on the importance of social and national harmony. Paradoxically, however, the Confucian concept of filial piety has generated a discussion in certain Asian societies about the extent to which, in their increasingly westernized cultural milieu, legislation may be required to impose a duty on children (whose devotion to this admirable virtue appears to be flagging) to provide financial assistance to their elderly parents.

It is undeniable that the universal adoption and advocacy of international human rights has reduced the warmth that Walzer and other theorists entreat us to adopt towards indigenous norms, values and culture. This is despite the ambiguity and incoherence of the concept of human rights, as mentioned in Chapter 8.

(Indeed, one might equally complain about the fuzziness of the concept of 'community'.) It may be too late to turn back; the 'globalization' of human rights stimulated by the United Nations and other international conventions and instruments vigorously supports the recognition of such rights in diverse societies and cultures, as we shall see in the following chapter.

Summing up

The starting point of communitarian theories is the Aristotelean notion that man is a 'social animal' and hence that the community is the most important component of a society or culture. Communitarians argue that we all belong to a community that develops our identity and relationships. They dislike the individualism of liberalism, preferring to advocate a more vigorous civic life and a more dynamic spirit of community. They generally believe that the ideals of autonomy, universality, detachment and natural rights undermine traditional communal values of solidarity and social responsibility. They also attach importance to devotion or loyalty to the community, family or workplace rather than to one's individual interests or rights.

Liberals criticize communitarians on a number of grounds, for example that the theory restricts the opportunity for individuals to choose what lives to lead and to advance their subjective ideas of development and self-fulfilment. While it may be true that extreme libertarianism, as for instance advanced by Robert Nozick, may undermine community values, the more moderate liberal defence of individual autonomy and rights would seem to provide some protection against moral relativism and an endorsement of the repressive policies of some societies.

12
Global justice

Should our concern for justice end at our border? Is injustice abroad not a legitimate moral concern? As frontiers melt away, the geographical divide between the rich and poor, unjust discrepancies in access to education, housing and sanitation, the threat of terrorism and the horrors of dictatorships, ethnic cleansing and genocide are closer to home than ever. The world has shrunk: air travel, 24-hour world news coverage, the Internet and social media have seen to that. The flood of migrants from war, persecution and poverty creates difficult challenges for governments, especially in Europe. Can these problems be resolved without significant international co-operation? Is military intervention justified to end genocide or grave violations of human rights? Is it legitimate for nations to close their frontiers to protect their security or their values? Is economic globalization fair to impoverished countries? What of the threat of climate change? Should our concern about justice extend to the protection of the environment and the threats to the habitat of tribes in the Amazon? What about the suffering of non-human creatures, who endure cruelty in many countries?

The problems are enormous: corruption, economic stagnation, civil conflict, little or no access to clean water, health care and the inequitable distribution of natural resources. These challenges are compounded by the population explosion in developing countries, which represents a very real challenge to the world's resources, stability and security. In Africa, to take one of the most disquieting examples, according to the United Nations 2015 report, *World Population Prospects*, by the end of this century the population could reach as many as six billion, an astonishing increase from its current 1.2 billion. The report adds that since African women give birth to an average of 4.7 children, the population is increasing nearly three times more quickly than in the rest of the world. Unless birth rates slow, the impact of this boom is likely to place enormous stress on resources. Any initiative to address this must, at the very least, empower women, especially through education but also politically, economically and socially, to expand their role beyond the home. And unless humans can learn to adapt to this growth by making better use of the earth's finite resources, competition can only grow. There are some signs of change; across the globe the average woman gives birth to 2.5 offspring. This is half as many as in the early 1950s. The fertility rate in forty percent of the world is at or below the 'replacement level' (the figure at which children take the place of their parents) of 2.1 children per woman.

Poor soil, an inadequate supply of clean water, unemployment and corrupt governments are a noxious cocktail that threatens peace and security beyond the continent. As a growing number of Africans migrate in search of better lives, the impact on the world, its resources and stability becomes evident. The vast, ignored inequalities in access to healthcare and the infectious diseases (such as malaria) that have still to be prevented or effectively treated add to the gloomy future faced by poorer nations. It is dreadful that such injustice should exist in the twenty-first century. The discrepancies between life expectancy across the globe are spectacular. The average Japanese woman can expect to die at the age of 87. Her counterpart in Sierra Leone is unlikely to live beyond the age of 46.

But we must not be dispirited or discouraged. Injustice is not inevitable. While poverty and disease continue to bedevil many countries, particularly in Africa and Asia, strides are being made to address these problems. At the beginning of this century the United Nations launched eight Millennium Development Goals (MDGs), adopted by all members of the world body. They are to:

1. Eradicate extreme poverty and hunger
2. Achieve universal primary education
3. Promote gender equality and empower women
4. Reduce child mortality
5. Improve maternal health
6. Combat HIV/AIDS, malaria and other diseases
7. Ensure environmental sustainability
8. Develop a global partnership for development

In 2015 these MDGs were replaced by the Sustainable Development Goals (SDGs) that commit the signatories to an even more ambitious set of seventeen objectives that include ending poverty in all its forms everywhere, promoting health, sustainable agriculture, education, access to water, energy, economic growth, productive employment and safe cities and human settlements. The emphasis is on sustainability, so the goals also identify the need for sustainable consumption, urgent action to combat climate change and conservation of terrestrial and marine ecosystems. In addition, the document includes the requirement to provide 'peaceful and inclusive societies for sustainable development ... access to justice for all and build effective, accountable and inclusive institutions at all levels'.

The achievement of these goals calls for considerable co-operation, commitments and cost but it represents a positive, reassuring recognition of the need for action. Whether they are too numerous or too diffuse remains to be seen. Ending this injustice will not be easy. But the wretchedness of so many cannot be allowed to continue.

ACCESS TO EDUCATION

The United Nations Children's Emergency Fund (UNICEF) reports that more than fifty-nine million children of primary school age are denied their right to education. Rather than declining, that figure has been increasing in recent years.

Sub-Saharan Africa accounts for more than a half of all out-of-school children worldwide, fifty-five percent of whom are girls. The agency states that 'without doubt' the world will not meet its most recent education goal. The current financial crisis has put extra pressure on strained public funding. The aid to education has fallen by ten percent since 2010. Should these funds become scarcer, access to education will continue to stagnate and the quality of schools will decline, denying the world's most vulnerable children a fundamental human right without which their future opportunities are dramatically limited.

The UNICEF data shows that thirty-six percent of all out-of-school children live in countries that have been affected by conflict. Most are children from the poorest families, from rural areas or from ethnic or linguistic minorities. Many are children with disabilities or children who have to work to help their families make ends meet. But the greatest challenge is faced by children with multiple disadvantages: girls from poor rural areas, ethnic minorities, children with disabilities and refugee children.

We routinely face these and countless associated questions that afflict our world. The migrant crisis in Europe, which is likely to continue for many years, raises complex questions about how to determine who is a genuine asylum seeker and the morality of closing borders to those fleeing war, poverty or persecution. There is also a plethora of challenges related to the demands for the greater protection of human rights, the recognition of the right to self-determination and whether democratic principles are exportable to countries in which they are alien or even reviled.

States and justice

The Peace of Westphalia in 1648, which ended the hugely destructive Thirty Years' War in central Europe, is generally considered to be the beginning of the modern era. This 'war' was actually a succession of extremely devastating wars between 1618 and 1648 that led to millions of civilian deaths from starvation and disease.

From this destructive conflict emerged the concept of sovereign nation-states, the territorial integrity of nations and the end of the idea of countries as the personal property of their monarchs. Our increasingly globalized world has witnessed a momentous decline in the importance of the nation state. Multinational corporations, regional associations such as the European Union, non-national networks such as the Internet, and the interlocking of national economies have substantially weakened its foundations. This interconnectedness has significant implications for what is now called global justice: injustice that either touches inhabitants of more than one state or where a matter cannot be resolved without their assistance or collaboration.

Globalization is multi-dimensional. Its most conspicuous features include the trans-nationally integrated economy that is dominated by companies whose tentacles reach beyond the frontiers of several states and that are regulated (more or less) by supranational institutions such as the World Trade Organization. These corporations are generally dedicated to the elimination of barriers to free trade and to greater degrees of economic and financial interdependence. The morality, or otherwise, of this seemingly overwhelming phenomenon raises a number of thorny questions: what kinds of economic arrangements are just? Should our international institutions be reformed to safeguard fair terms of co-operation in our globalized world? Can globalization be better managed so that it works to assist the global poor more effectively? Are protectionist policies in trade justified or is free trade required by considerations of justice? Should poor working conditions in developing countries be a matter of concern for citizens and consumers in affluent, developed countries? If so, how might harmful employment conditions be effectively improved?

Yet again, we must turn John Rawls. He describes his book, *The Law of Peoples*, as 'an extension of a liberal conception of justice for a domestic regime to a Society of Peoples'. When he refers to 'peoples', Rawls means nations. This therefore amounts to an attempt to apply the ideas we discussed in Chapter 5 to international relations. He expounds eight principles that ought to apply to this situation: the recognition of nations' independence and equality, their right to self-determination as well as their duty of non-intervention, the duty to abide by treaties, respect certain human rights, conform to applicable norms when they engage in warfare and to assist in forming institutions to facilitate nations' self-determination.

You will recall that Rawls's difference principle seeks to put a brake on inequality. It specifies that all inequalities in the distribution of social primary goods must be justified as being in the interests of the worst-off members of society. In the case of global justice, however, his position is more measured. Justice in the international context would require nations to treat one another fairly but without any kind of distributive concern or claim for economic fairness. This disparity has, not surprisingly, attracted disapproval. It reveals, several critics claim, an inconsistency between his anxieties about domestic inequality and his apparent toleration of the enormous gap between rich and poor nations.

The extent to which Rawls's ideas in *A Theory of Justice* can be transplanted into the international arena has been doubted, especially by Nussbaum, who questions his analogy between states and the people in the original position. She is (rightly) sceptical about whether many governments actually have the interests of their people at heart. Nor is she persuaded by his assumption of the legitimacy of the status quo in many nations; they often lack accountability. Third, his account presumes the self-sufficiency of states, which neglects the significance of supra-national organizations and the interdependence between states in the modern world. His contractarian approach, she claims, is an unhelpful and impractical attempt to meet the demands of global justice.

None of these deficiencies are properly resolved in *The Law of Peoples* because Rawls is silent about the numerous challenges generated by multi-national agreements, institutions and agencies, the fluctuating patterns of the world economic order or the role of non-governmental organizations (NGOs), political movements and other groups that influence public policy, often without regard for national frontiers. One example of his alleged impractical outlook is his discussion of immigration which, he asserts, would disappear if all nations had proper governance. The conditions that frequently lead people to migrate – instability, corruption, lack of jobs and economic growth – might well be improved by better governance, although it is doubtful that it would cause immigration to disappear altogether. He identifies some of these sources of migration – religious and ethnic persecution, political oppression, famine and population pressure – maintaining that they are susceptible to control by domestic policy. Yet he neglects some of the major causes of emigration: economic inequality, malnutrition, sickness and lack of education, which are frequently linked to poverty. This criticism is echoed by other theorists. Why, it is asked, should territory define moral duty? In any event, since the people in the original position behind the veil of ignorance do not know to which society they belong, the principles of justice they select must surely apply to all societies!

Thomas Pogge (1953–) perceives global poverty to be a malevolent consequence of international institutions established by rich nations and imposed on the poor, whose right to be free from harm is, in effect, violated. He shows how global inequality in wealth or power is often transformed into openings for exploitation when rich countries deploy their authority to influence the rules and procedures of international trade and investment, emasculating the capacity of inhabitants of faraway countries to lead decent lives. He cites the example of the International Borrowing and Resource Privileges that allow governments to borrow funds, thereby incurring an obligation on the country to repay the debt. These privileges enable a government to use the money as it pleases and even sell the privileges at a price of its choosing. Moreover, any group wielding effective power in a state is treated as the legitimate government of that territory and receives these privileges. This, Pogge argues, creates objectionable inducements that impede the development of poor countries. Fraud, corruption and coups are accordingly encouraged; political office becomes an appealing means by which to acquire wealth. The venality of political leaders of many developing nations is a major obstruction not only to economic progress but also to the protection of human rights and the pursuit of justice.

These are fair points, though one can see why strong, stable institutions and political values are central to the Rawlsian ideal. In the absence of a robust political culture with institutions that respect the rule of law, the separation of powers, and other features taken for granted in most democratic societies, the prospects for justice are seriously diminished. For Rawls, as long as all nations have institutions that permit citizens to lead decent lives, moral anxieties about inequality between nations are trivial.

Duties to strangers?

How far do our obligations extend? Do Italians owe moral duties to Indians or Belgians to Brazilians? A nationalist might legitimately claim that, like charity, justice begins at home. Is our primary responsibility towards our disadvantaged compatriots?

Or as human beings are we morally obliged to extend care and concern to our fellow human beings? For Pogge, since humans shape and manage global organizations, their commitment to justice should transcend national borders and extend their concern to all inhabitants of the world. Nor is there any reason why local and global consideration cannot co-exist. Indeed it is arguable that justice at an international level has an impact on encouraging fairness domestically.

Other critics have reservations about the moral equivalence of international trade on the one hand and the relationship between individuals who are members of a particular nation on the other. Is trading in goods and services really comparable to the sort of co-operation that exists between citizens? There is much in Thomas Nagel's (1937–) argument that distributive justice, in the absence of a world government with powers akin to a sovereign state, is not feasible. We may owe moral duties to the poor but they are *humanitarian* obligations. You cannot achieve distributive justice without coercive political institutions to do the distributing in the name of the people. Such institutions are largely absent from the international sphere, although some theorists argue that coercion in the international realm exists when powerful nations invade foreign nations, stealthily remove delinquent governments or control their borders.

Your nationality is an accident of birth. It is no different from your class, race and sex. Why then, Pogge asks, applying the logic of Rawlsian principles of justice, would those behind the veil of ignorance not regard themselves as representing human beings *everywhere*? This would result in agreement on a catalogue of human rights that would include a system of international economic limitations and principles relating to the redistribution of natural resources. Indeed, Charles Beitz (1949–) argues that natural resources resemble natural talents; they should not be considered to be the property of the state within whose borders they happen to be situated. Since, as Rawls maintains, individuals may use their talents but they do not have an unqualified right to the profit derived therefrom, natural resources may similarly be used to benefit the least well-off.

Could this work? Nussbaum is doubtful. She points to the critical differences between persons and peoples. The individuals envisaged by Rawls who pick principles of justice are a different proposition from nation states. Those behind the veil of ignorance are roughly equal in basic economic productivity and life chances, before the exigencies of life kick in. And that occurs after birth, after factors such as differential nutrition, cognitive stimulation, disparities in maternal nutrition, health care, emotional well-being and HIV status have already had their impact. Moreover, as she mentions, there is not even equality in respect of the opportunity to be born: sex-selective abortion in many developing countries results in girls having wholly unequal life chances. Her point is that these inequalities between nations dictate that certain nations be excluded in order to conform to Rawls's concept of justice. These inequalities are transformed into inequities among persons in respect of their intrinsic, indelible life chances. This attempt at global social contractarianism departs substantially from a Rawlsian framework, because it requires abandoning his notion that the people in the original position are seeking to strike a deal to achieve mutual advantage among those who are roughly equal.

An alternative?

This rejection of Rawls's answer leads Nussbaum to propose what she calls a 'co-operative' scheme that, you will not be surprised to discover, is founded on the capabilities approach advanced by her and Amartya Sen (see Chapter 7). Preferring a 'richer' form of pre-contractarianism ideas of collaboration in the natural law tradition, she draws on the writings of Hugo de Groot, or 'Grotius' as he is known (1583–1645), who is commonly associated with the secularization of natural law. In his influential work *De Jure Belli ac Pacis* he asserts that even if God did not exist ('*etiamsi daremus non esse Deum*') the content of natural law would not change. This was a significant basis for the emerging discipline of public international law, although it is not entirely clear what Grotius means by his *etiamsi daremus* notion. I believe that he is claiming that certain things are 'intrinsically' wrong, whether or not they are decreed by God. To employ Grotius's own analogy, even God cannot cause two times two to equal something other than four. Grotius does not repudiate God's existence, he merely declares that what is right or wrong are questions of natural rightness, not of arbitrary divine *fiat*.

We want, Nussbaum, maintains, to inhabit a world in which everyone has access to what they need to live a life with dignity. The capabilities approach, you will remember, is based on *outcomes*; it states that a world in which people enjoy all the capabilities that feature on her list is a minimally just and decent world. In the case of a single nation, it understands the goal of social co-operation to be that of establishing principles and institutions that ensure that individuals either possess the listed capabilities or, if they do not, can effectively claim them. It is therefore closely related to domestic institutional and constitutional design.

But what about its application globally? We have a shared responsibility to ensure that people everywhere receive their due: human dignity. We need to ask, she says, what is required to live a fully human life, one that is worthy of the dignity of a human being. Fundamentally this includes co-operation between humans to fulfil our needs, which include adequate nutrition, education, protection of bodily integrity, freedom of speech and religion and other liberties. If humans have these needs, there is a consequential obligation to provide it to all the people of the world. How? The capabilities approach requires that special efforts need to be made to address the unequal requirements of those who begin from a position of social disadvantage. Our objective is not merely 'negative liberty' but the complete facility of people to be and to choose these capabilities that all have an *economic* dimension: they cost money. Even freedom of speech requires education, adequate nutrition and so on.

The approach challenges the idea of development as economic growth, favouring instead the notion of *'human development'*. We must address the problem of how to assign the burdens of promoting the capabilities in a globalized world governed by international economic agreements and agencies and multi-national corporations. Since it is people who control institutions, it is they who bear the moral duty to advance human capabilities for at least three reasons. First, a proper institutional structure should be established and then individuals may delegate their moral duties to those institutions, both domestically and globally. Second, there is the matter of fairness: voluntary philanthropy is unfair on those who give, unless others pay their fair share and there is a system that ensures this, the altruistic end up giving more. Third, unless a utilitarian position is rejected (in which people are merely engines of maximization), individuals will lose their identity, integrity, agency and hence their human dignity.

To repeat, the solution is to assign the responsibility for promoting others' well-being or capabilities to *institutions*, allowing individuals wide discretion about how to live their lives. Institutions have the merit of fairly imposing on all the duty to support the capabilities of everyone, up to a minimum threshold. Individuals are left free to use their time, wealth and other resources to pursue their own concept of the good.

Within a state the institutions responsible for maintaining citizens' capabilities will be found in the constitution. They include the legislature, executive and judiciary, as well as the legal and economic systems. Globally, however, the position is less obvious.

There is no over-arching sovereign world state. Nor would such a structure satisfy the demands of accountability; cultural and linguistic differences would always render communication difficult. Such a 'state' already exists, she suggests, based in part on the domestic structures to which the obligation could be assigned to redistribute some of the wealth to other nations. It will include multi-national corporations, which might be allocated the duty to promote human capabilities in those nations where they do business. Part of the 'state' will consist of global economic policies, agencies and agreements, including the World Bank, the International Monetary Fund, various trade agreements, international bodies, such as the United Nations, the International Labour Organization, the International Court of Justice, the International Criminal Court and international treaties and covenants on several subjects, such as human rights, labour and the environment. Another part will comprise NGOs.

She proposes ten principles to govern this global structure and foster capabilities in an unequal world. They include the duty of prosperous nations to give a substantial portion of their GDP to poorer nations. The figure of one percent is 'morally adequate'. Whether it should be given directly to governments or also directly to NGOs is unclear; the general principle would be not to weaken national sovereignty if the recipient nation is democratic but to contribute efficiently and in a manner that respects the capabilities on the list. Another principle is that multi-national corporations should advance human capabilities in the regions in which they operate; they must devote a substantial proportion of their profits to improving education and the environment. Such measures are in their own interests: corporations benefit from a stable, well-educated workforce and political stability; a proper educational system encourages political engagement, which is vital for the health of a democracy. A further principle recommends that the key structures of the global economic system should be designed to be fair to poor and developing countries. Another suggestion is for the creation of a decentralized, yet dynamic, global public sphere that would include global environmental regulations, with enforcement mechanisms and a tax on the industrial nations of the north to support the development of pollution controls in the south; a set of global trade regulations that establish moral goals for human development, global labour standards for both the formal and the informal sector, enforced by sanctions and a limited form of global taxation that would transfer wealth from richer to poorer nations. The principles would also contain an explicit obligation to care for the ill, the elderly and the disabled. The family should be protected, including the freedom to choose to marry and found a family. Special emphasis should be placed on the needs of the disadvantaged and the importance of education in empowering them.

It is hard to criticize this approach, however utopian it may appear. It springs from a deep anxiety about global injustice, especially the poverty that leads, for example, to nine million deaths annually in the developing world from (mainly preventable) infectious diseases. The comparable figure in the developed world is just 20,000. This disparity is indefensible. At the heart of the emphasis on capabilities is the destructive impact of these sorts of inequalities on human dignity.

Compassion and care are unquestionably critical values but should victims look to the global community for relief? Nagel, as we saw, contends that they should not: 'actual justice cannot be achieved except within a sovereign state'. A starving individual in Bangladesh is owed duties by his government and his compatriots but not by those who are not fellow inhabitants of Bangladesh. Humanitarianism is one thing but actual obligations to improve the lot of others beyond one's borders are another. Perhaps a clearer answer may emerge by briefly looking at just two of the many urgent and contentious problems currently facing the world.

Migration

The current migrant crisis has seen more than a million individuals from a variety of countries flee war, persecution or poverty to seek refuge or opportunity in Europe. The European Commission has predicted that three million migrants could arrive in the European Union by 2017. According to the United Nations High Commissioner for Refugees (UNHCR) the number of forcibly displaced people across the globe reached almost sixty million by the end of 2014. The number has since grown. Of these, some nineteen million were refugees from three countries: Syria (forty-nine percent), Afghanistan (twenty-one percent) and Iraq (eight percent). This influx poses enormous challenges to European governments and the European Union. Numerous difficult problems arise, including how to define a 'refugee' and the moral duties owed to both genuine refugees and so-called 'economic' migrants. From a justice perspective the central question boils down to whether, to stem the influx, a state has the right to close its borders and, if so, on what grounds. The most compelling arguments in support of closed borders are cultural, economic, political and benefits-related. They combine to make the case for national sovereignty trumping humanitarianism. The opposing argument in support of open borders typically relies on the right to freedom of movement and to equality of opportunity.

Open or closed borders?

The contention is increasingly heard that every nation is entitled to preserve, protect and defend its cultural, moral and religious values. A number of European states have invoked this claim to justify closing their borders to the many thousands who wish to enter their territory either to gain access to other countries or to seek asylum. It is argued that migrants from Islamic countries generally espouse beliefs and practices that are fundamentally hostile or inimical to the principles of Western societies, religious or secular. The philosopher Bruce Ackerman (1943–) asserts: 'The *only* reason for restricting immigration is to protect the ongoing process of liberal conversation itself'. In other words, those who are committed to the destruction of 'liberal conversation' may justifiably be excluded. Michael Walzer goes further and defends the right of *any* society to safeguard its cultural distinctiveness. But how can we test the soundness or intensity of this alleged threat from Muslim migrants? We obviously require some sort of persuasive evidence that the new arrivals will resist assimilation. Is the indication that this has occurred in country X sufficient proof that it is likely to occur in other countries? Can we be sure that the threat is real and negative? Is the argument against migrants irrational, based largely on prejudice or racism?

From a justice point of view, does the right of a state to preserve its distinctive culture or religion translate into a moral right to exclude refugees? Do the rights of citizens to preserve their cultural identity eclipse the rights of foreigners to enter their land? These rights, a libertarian might assert, plainly include the migrant's right to freedom of movement and, for example, an employer's freedom of contract: his right to employ the individual of his choice. Freedom of movement is not an unrestricted right; you cannot enter my property without my consent, so why should the migrant have a right to enter my country? On the other hand, the law determines the nature and extent of my property rights, so one might argue that – equally – immigration law can trump individuals' rights to land.

But what of the rights of foreigners? As we discussed in Chapter 7, the accident of birth often endows an individual with a cluster of positive life chances. If we take equality seriously, should it matter whether Ben was born in Burkina Faso or Brenda in Bulgaria? Luck is crucial; it sets you on a path you cannot choose and will be key in determining how you judge the world and its inhabitants, as captured in the current mantra: 'check your privilege'. One way to try to close the gap between rich and poor is to open borders. But it is not easy to persuade a government to forego its territorial integrity and, instead of locking the gates, reach for their wallets and assist poor nations through aid. There is also the legitimate dread of terrorist attacks committed by Islamist groups such as ISIS, Al-Qaeda, the Taliban, Boko Haram and Al-Shabaab. Border controls can never totally deter extremists who are bent on committing murderous atrocities. Eradicating immigration would still permit guest workers, students, tourists and others on brief stays – who may be terrorists – to enter the country.

Another argument is that unrestricted entry affects citizens' access to benefits, welfare payments and health insurance. A welfare state that fails to limit immigration is a magnet for the poor, which would adversely affect the entitlements of residents lawfully residing in the country. One compromise, currently under consideration in Britain, is to delay the right to welfare for a number of years. Another is to tax the income of migrants immediately on their arrival so that only when they had contributed sufficiently to the welfare system would they be able to claim benefits.

The negative effects of immigration on schools, hospitals, housing and other public services is another complaint, along with the claim that migrants harm the economy, drive down wages, cause locals to lose their jobs and, because of the dissimilar culture of new workers, hinder economic growth. On the other hand, it is arguable that migrants provide cheaper labour and hence help lower consumer prices. It is also asserted that the free movement of labour benefits the global economy. It is unlikely that the difficulties engendered by the large flow of migrants to Europe will diminish for many years, if not decades, to come.

The environment

Our world also faces a host of environmental challenges that directly affect global justice. These range from the destruction of habitats, breaking down of the ozone layer, deforestation and the ever-increasing rate of extinction of species. It is, however, the apparent perils of climate change that have attracted the greatest international attention and concern. Despite the absence of unanimity on the subject, the scientific evidence overwhelmingly points ineluctably to anthropogenic climate change being a genuine and serious threat to the planet.

At the 2015 UN Climate Change Conference, held in Paris, the representatives of 196 parties agreed to set a goal of limiting global warming to less than two degrees Celsius above pre-industrial levels. It called for zero net anthropogenic greenhouse gas emissions to be reached by the second half of this century. The participants also undertook to pursue efforts to limit the temperature increase to 1.5° Celsius which, they believed, will require zero emissions between 2030 and 2050. The agreement will become legally binding when at least fifty-five countries that together represent the source of at least fifty-five percent of global greenhouse gas emissions sign between April 2016 and April 2017 and also ratify it domestically.

One troubling snag is the fact that many poor countries rely on the burning of fossil fuels to generate energy; this is considered a major cause of climate change. Can a bargain be struck between rich and poor nations to facilitate a just and equitable solution to this problem? Some have suggested that the cost should fall on those advanced industrialized nations that have contributed most to global warming. But is this principle ('the polluter pays') just? It presumes that these countries were *aware* of the damage they were inflicting on the planet when their smokestacks were belching greenhouse gases into the air. Since it was not until about 1990 that scientists discovered a definitive link between greenhouse gases and climate change, a fairer standard in respect of post-1990 emissions is 'the beneficiary pays' principle. This has the moral attraction that it attaches responsibility to the benefit or advantage that the country in question has actually accrued. Nevertheless, even this approach seems morally unsound: why should past transgressions innocently committed justify a sanction merely because of the benefit enjoyed? Perhaps the fairest approach is to adopt 'the ability to pay' principle; it looks to the deepest pockets to bear the cost of limiting the consequences of the depredations to the earth.

Another injustice associated with the environment is the intentional or unintentional location of hazardous waste sites in or close to residential areas that are predominantly inhabited by minority racial groups or the poor. Sometimes regarded as an element of what has come to be called 'environmental racism' it comprises a variety of phenomena that include the disproportionate adverse effects of certain environmental policies, such as the differential rate of removal of environmental contaminants in poorer communities, compelling workers to choose between hazardous jobs and accepted health and safety standards and the lack of access to, or the unsatisfactory upkeep of, public parks and playgrounds.

A world government?

The vision of some form of global regime is not new. The dream is of a democratic mechanism with the capacity to end war, poverty and injustice. Dante, Hobbes, Kant and Rousseau have, on different grounds and in varying degrees, imagined an over-arching world power that might foster what Kant called 'perpetual peace'. Kant advocated the formation of a peaceful world community, not, strictly speaking, a global government but an organ to pursue the ideal of a peaceful world in which nations would declare themselves free states, respecting their citizens and opening their doors to foreign visitors as fellow rational beings.

How plausible is the idea of an actual world government exercising authority over all nations, especially in the light of the vigorous defence of sovereignty evinced by most states and the challenge of establishing an institutional structure that would be acceptable to the almost two hundred countries of the world? What of the world's diversity of cultures, values and ways of life? Some argue that they could be supressed in the name of uniform unity.

The world succeeded in establishing the United Nations and its (ineffectual) predecessor, the League of Nations (whose failure is generally attributed to several factors, including its limited membership and powers and international instability). International governmental organizations (IGOs) range in size from three to more than 185 members (for example, the UN) and their geographical representation ranges from a single region (the European Union) to all regions (such as the International Monetary Fund). Their functions obviously differ; the principal function of the North Atlantic Treaty Organization (NATO) is to safeguard the freedom and security of its members by political and military means, whereas the International Labour Organization (ILO) is mainly concerned with protecting the interests of workers. These bodies provide an important forum for discussion, debate and even, occasionally, resolution of international conflict. They clearly play an important role in fostering international co-operation, the collection, analysis and dissemination of information and the setting of internationally acceptable norms. But they fall far short of the vision of an authentic international administration with the powers and duties of a genuine government, including centralized control, the authority to enforce the peaceful settlement of disputes and disarmament at state and regional levels and the global legislative capacity sustained by enforcement mechanisms.

Rawls, in *The Law of Peoples,* sketches the concept of a society of peoples, governed by principles that foster co-operative associations among peoples, that stops short of a world-state. He echoes Kant's misgivings about the creation of such a body that could become repressive or generate 'civil strife' as states seek to achieve political autonomy. Ironically, Rawls's other great work, *A Theory of Justice*, has been deployed by among others Pogge and Beitz in support of an international liberal community along the lines of the domestic project he describes. This so-called 'moral cosmopolitanism' does not, however, recommend a world government but a global moral community that recognizes the equal value of people. It is a somewhat romantic idyll to which we can all subscribe, though its realization seems as remote as ever in the contemporary riven and unstable world. Far more promising is the prospect of a reformed, effectively administered, United Nations. Following Rawls, Pogge acknowledges the need for universal institutions with increased powers to supersede the sovereignty of states. This requires, he argues, progress towards a world in which the majority of states are stable democracies.

An obsessive – but often understandable – defence of state sovereignty is plainly a critical impediment to a genuinely peaceful world order, although the establishment of the International Criminal Court (ICC) in 1998 represents a scintilla of hope among the gloom of sovereign possessiveness. Governed by the Rome Statute that came into force on 1 July 2002, the court is the first permanent, treaty-based, international tribunal established to try individuals, including heads of state, for genocide, war crimes and crimes against humanity. The court in The Hague is independent of the UN and is largely funded by the states that are party to the Rome Statute. Its creation marks a significant recognition that impunity for international crimes is no longer tolerable. Its jurisdiction is, however, restricted by the concept of 'complementarity': the court can only prosecute an offender when domestic courts fail to do so. It therefore poses no threat to the sovereignty of local judiciaries.

JUSTICE ON TRIAL

Tribunals to try those responsible for various injustices are a significant development. After the Second World War the Nuremberg International Military Tribunal was founded to prosecute Nazi war criminals. The court established the important precedent that individuals could be held criminally liable for crimes under international law. Several of those convicted were sentenced to death. This laid the foundation for the establishment of other international courts, such as the International Criminal Court for the Former Yugoslavia and the International Criminal Tribunal for Rwanda.

The International Criminal Court

The International Criminal Court (ICC) is a permanent institution created by a treaty, the Rome Statute, which came into force on 1 July 2002. It is a court of 'last resort', with jurisdiction over 'the most serious crimes of international concern', namely, genocide, crimes against humanity, war crimes and aggression committed after the statute entered into force. At the time of writing, thirty-nine leaders have been indicted but only three have been successfully convicted, all from the Democratic Republic of Congo.

The ICC is not without its critics. Progress is slow and the conviction rate is low. It has been accused of bias, particularly by the African Union, for its focus on Africa.

At the time of writing, the Rome Statute has been ratified (formally adopted by the legislature of the country) by 124 states. Another thirty-four, including Israel, Iran and Egypt, have signed and may ratify it in the future. The most conspicuous omission is the United States, which has expressed the fear that its troops might be the subject of politically motivated or frivolous prosecutions and withdrawn its intent to ratify. The Bush administration was obdurate in its opposition to the court, even threatening to withdrawn from the UN force in Bosnia unless it was granted immunity from prosecution by the ICC. Other countries have still not signed the treaty, let alone ratified it; these include China, Pakistan, India, Indonesia and Turkey. Late 2016 saw a disturbing development. A number of African countries (including South Africa, Burundi, and Gambia) decided to withdraw from the ICC accusing it of seeking only to prosecute Africans. This was followed by an announcement that Russia would no longer accept the jurisdiction of the court, claiming that the tribunal had failed to live up to hopes of the international community and denouncing its work as "one-sided and inefficient".

Of course, the justice involved and dispensed by the court relates to criminal justice. There is still no global mechanism by which distributive justice might be achieved. Its advocates show little sign of abandoning their campaign.

Summing up

Our increasingly globalised world and the expansion in the number of international institutions raise far-reaching questions about our moral and political obligations beyond domestic borders. To achieve justice, the evils of poverty, disease, civil conflict, environmental degradation, corruption and terrorism are just some of the grave challenges that must be overcome. Despite efforts made by intergovernmental organisations such as the United Nations, NATO and the G20 (Group of Twenty) states to tackle these cross-border issues, the concept of a world government remains a utopian ideal. Nevertheless, these dangers cannot be successfully tackled without a high degree of international co-operation on the part of the richest and most powerful nations of the world and the involvement of the poorest countries.

13 Achieving social justice

The concept of justice – like the competing theories that attempt to capture its features – is always contentious. And the means by which to create a society or a world in which all inhabitants can live under conditions of fairness, equality and mutual respect is no less so. Individuals and groups in many societies suffer discrimination, hostility and hatred. Intolerance is the antithesis of justice and compassion. Members of the LGBT community are subject to enmity, punishment and even death. Homosexuality remains unlawful in some seventy-six countries including Egypt, Iran, Afghanistan and Singapore. Gay people face punishment ranging from forced psychiatric treatment and lifelong prison sentences to hard labour and killing by public stoning. Abuse of women, racism, anti-Semitism, prejudice and bigotry are on the rise around the world. Religious freedom is under serious threat in many Islamic and South-East Asian countries. Egypt's Christian Coptic minority, the Baha'is in Iran, the Ahmadis in Pakistan, and Christians, Hindus, Buddhists and Shi'i Muslims in Saudi Arabia are among the world's most repressed religious minorities.

RELIGIOUS PERSECUTION

In its 2016 report the United States Commission on International Religious Freedom (USCIRF) placed eight nations, Central African Republic, Egypt, Iraq, Nigeria, Pakistan, Syria, Tajikistan and Vietnam, on its list of 'countries of particular concern' (CPC), defined as those where particularly severe violations of religious freedom are tolerated or perpetrated. It also recommended that nine further countries be designated CPCs: Burma, China, Eritrea, Iran, North Korea, Saudi Arabia, Sudan, Turkmenistan and Uzbekistan. Ten more were described as countries whose governments engage in or tolerate at least one of the elements of the 'systematic, ongoing and egregious' standard but do not fully meet the CPC standard: Afghanistan, Azerbaijan, Cuba, India, Indonesia, Kazakhstan, Laos, Malaysia, Russia and Turkey. Other countries monitored include Bahrain, Bangladesh, Belarus, countries in the Horn of Africa and Kyrgyzstan.

Around the world, some 795 million people are estimated to be undernourished. Indefensibly, today more than ninety million children under the age of five are underfed and underweight. The World Health Organization reports that in 2015, 5.9 million children died before reaching their fifth birthday. That is – astonishingly – 16,000 deaths every day. However, the UN also found that under-five mortality rate has *decreased* by fifty-three percent from an estimated rate of ninety-one deaths per one thousand live births in 1990 to forty-three deaths per one thousand live births in 2015. Approximately 19,000 fewer children died every day in 2015 than in 1990, the baseline year for measuring progress. None the less, the disparity between child mortality in high-income and low-income countries remains great. The under-five mortality rate is highest in Africa (eighty-one per one thousand live births), more than seven times higher than the rate in Europe (eleven per one thousand live births) and eleven times higher than the average rate in high-income countries (seven deaths per one thousand live births). In 1820, average life expectancy around the world was just twenty-six and rose to only thirty-one by 1900. According to the United Nations it is now seventy-one years.

It is astonishing that in the twenty-first century slavery still exists but it is a widespread, intractable concern. It is estimated by the third Global Slavery Index that there may be as many as forty-six million slaves in the world today. Modern slavery is a major industry, generating up to $35 billion per year. It has been suggested that India has some 18 million slaves, China 3.4 million and Pakistan more than 2 million. In North Korea and Uzbekistan more than four percent of the population is enslaved.

A dramatic example of inequality is the caste system in India, which entrenches sharp divisions between members of different communities. For some groups, discrimination is practised in respect of numerous aspects of life. The so-called 'untouchables' (the self-chosen term is 'Dalit') are restricted to menial positions and employment, even though such discrimination is outlawed by the Indian constitution. The government has introduced a number of affirmative action measures to improve the lives of lower caste members. In 2007, India elected K.G. Balakrishnan, a Dalit, to the office of Chief Justice, followed in 2009 by another Dalit, Meira Kumar, who was unanimously elected by parliament as the first female speaker.

There are other glimmers of hope. World poverty has fallen more in the last half-century than it has in the preceding five centuries, according to the United Nations Development Programme. The World Bank only considers thirty-five countries to be 'low-income', although, globally, more than eight-hundred million people are still living in extreme poverty and as many as three-hundred million workers lived below the US$1.25 a day poverty line in 2015. For the first time since poverty trends began to be monitored, the number of people living in extreme poverty has declined in every developing region, including sub-Saharan

Africa, where rates are highest. According to the United Nations, more than a billion people have been lifted out of extreme poverty since 1990. In that year nearly half of the population in the developing regions of the world lived on less than US$1.25 a day. This dropped to fourteen percent in 2015. Only four out of ten young women and men aged fifteen to twenty-four were employed in 2015, compared with five out of ten in 1991.

What is a just society?

There is, as we have seen, a significant divergence of views concerning both its fundamental features and its soundest philosophical foundation. Can a Kantian ever agree with a utilitarian? Is a Rawlsian likely to see eye-to-eye with a communitarian? An aficionado of the capabilities approach and a Nozickean libertarian might as well inhabit different planets.

Who gets the flute?

Suppose there is a flute. Each of three children wants it. Aldo says he should have it because she is the only one who knows how to play. Bruno argues it should be his because he is poor and has no toys. Carlo, however, claims the right to the instrument because he made it. How do we decide between these three legitimate claims?

Bruno would win the support of the economic egalitarian. Carlo would have the backing of Nozick and libertarians. A utilitarian would attach importance to the pleasure that Aldo, the only flautist of the three, would derive from the flute but he would also recognize that Bruno's relative deprivation could render his incremental gain in happiness much greater from being awarded the flute. Each claim has its merits and its champions: the pursuit of human fulfilment (A), the elimination of poverty (B) and the entitlement to the fruits of one's labour (C). Other theories would attach different moral weight to each of the three demands.

Figure 2: *Portrait of Three Children, One Playing a Flute.* Guiseppe Assereto (c. 1626– c. 1657).

Is there no compromise that might be struck? Surely, there is a middle ground or consensus that could be reached? Do the numerous theories canvassed in this book share any essential convictions about the fundamental elements of justice and how to achieve a fair society? The notion of equality springs to mind. There is certainly an acknowledgement in all theories of the injustice of inequality. Similarly, the concepts of liberty and individual rights are generally embraced. Yet scratch the surface and beneath this ostensible concord lurk the deep-seated ideological and practical differences described in the preceding chapters. For instance, 'equality' is not only in itself a problematic concept but the manner of its practical social application – judicially, economically, politically – inescapably turns on the moral theory to which its advocate subscribes. We cannot, nor should not, expect unanimity, let alone consensus, when it comes to reflecting on the contours of an egalitarian society.

To take only one of many possible examples, the assault on Rawls that emanates from various quarters frequently stigmatizes his social contract as abstract, transcendental or morally and politically defective. This criticism, I suggest, seems to overlook the very problem that besets any attempt to arrive at a minimally settled conception of justice. The heuristic strategy of the 'original position' seems to me to be an adroit technique by which to establish a neutral framework that is critical to this demanding undertaking. You will, I hope, remember that the construct is presented in order to create a fair and neutral point of view to be adopted when the people in this position select fundamental principles of justice. They imagine themselves as free and equal people who mutually agree on principles of social and political justice. Its key element is the 'veil of ignorance', which ensures the objectivity and detachment of the participants who are stripped of all knowledge of their personal attributes and their social circumstances.

The powerful attack launched by Sen and Nussbaum on this construct (discussed in Chapter 7) is based on their entirely understandable concern to discuss what they see as the *practical* questions of justice and injustice. They express their impatience with theory which, they argue, does not adequately confront the grotesque injustices endured by many across the globe. Theirs is a noble, principled strategy that looks to actual policy outcomes rather than to the procedural preoccupations that they find unpalatable in social contractarianism. This impatience with analysis is a reasonable reaction to the horrors of gross poverty, various forms of persecution, terrorism and war that afflict our world. But it does not, as far as I can see, answer the, admittedly difficult, question of how to tackle the injustices also present in so many parts of the world. The two approaches have different objectives; the issue between them is never fully joined. The protagonists seem to be shadow boxing.

As you will have gathered, I am partial to the importance that Rawls attaches to just institutions. It is all very well to dispute the flute but in the absence of some equitable institutional arrangement, the competing claims of the three contenders will not receive proper consideration. The flute will stay silent. But although I place a high degree of trust in the fairness of democratic structures, they must be subject to relentless scrutiny, oversight and reform. 'Justice', Rawls rightly says, 'is the first virtue of social institutions'. Any plausible theory of justice should, I believe, propound a social structure that specifies how the principal institutions dispense justice. That is to say how they distribute fundamental rights, duties, benefits and burdens.

But even this paradigm is imperfect. A Rawlsian society, while it may alleviate, would not eliminate, injustice. Nor would it necessarily resolve the problems of how entitlement to property originally came about, discussed in Chapter 6, thwart corruption and control free market forces (Chapter 8), guarantee perfect equality (Chapter 9) or fully recognize the legitimate rights of women, the disabled and animals (Chapter 10). Its essentially individualist concept of the person would diverge from a communitarian interpretation of justice (Chapter 11) and its reach would not extend beyond its borders (Chapter 12). Rawls concedes as much. His theory, while ambitious in its rejection of utilitarian and intuitionist concepts of justice, is modest in its claim that the principles of justice are merely a part, albeit an important part, of a complete concept specifying criteria for all the virtues of the basic structure of society. He does, however, stress the value of social co-operation for reciprocal advantage. This is in keeping both with his Aristotelean belief that participation in the life of a well-ordered society is a great good and his Kantian defence of personal autonomy.

The value of Rawls's vision lies, I think, in this attempt to recognize and reconcile the distinctiveness of the individual on the one hand with the requirement of community consensus on the other. On its own, no theory can solve practical problems. Rawls does not claim otherwise. His is a philosophical answer to the classic question of what constitutes justice, not a manual for tackling injustice. Is there some method by which theory and practice can coalesce to enhance the prospects of social justice?

I return to my starting point, South Africa. Its transformation from apartheid state to constitutional democracy is a striking illustration of the possibilities of achieving justice. Its institutional revolution now promises universal franchise, free and fair elections and civil liberties and the protection of human rights, all buttressed by robust judicial protection of its famous democratic constitution. Free housing is provided to millions and water and electricity are accessible to the great majority of the population. A substantial black middle class has emerged, which drives the economy. Yet (although the law promotes affirmative action to mitigate the effects of inequality and huge rates of unemployment) enormous inequality, racism, high levels of crime, corruption and cronyism persist.

Governments across the world have committed themselves to the promotion of social justice at national, regional and international levels. Central to this undertaking is a more equitable distribution of income, equality of opportunity and the protection of human rights. One can only hope that these are not simply empty promises or noble aspirations. Every nation has the capacity to improve the prospects of justice for its inhabitants. Despite the suffering endured by many – seen as the media broadcast vivid images of the injustices of war, poverty and persecution on to our screens – there is evidence of greater tolerance and compassion in our world. Yet, while the solution to these challenges may appear straightforward, they require careful consideration and analysis. This is why a coherent idea of what actually constitutes social justice is so important. Efforts to tackle inequality and improve lives are essential but we need a clear idea of what we are seeking to achieve.

'There is nothing more practical than a good theory,' wrote the psychologist Kurt Lewin. A good theory of justice is a prerequisite both of specifying its features and measuring our progress towards its realization. There are practical issues to resolve but they must be based on a clearly-defined notion of justice. A theory can offer the foundation for rational agreement where sharp divisions may generate conflict and discord. It may also enable citizens to understand their social role and position and afford a vision of how their society might be improved. The preceding chapters provide an outline of the leading theories. Scrupulous reflection on these contending approaches is a vital means by which to further our quest to advance the cause of justice.

Some key terms

This is a brief list of the main terms that occur in the book, where they are discussed in much greater detail. They are here as a quick reminder of their meaning.

Aristocracy The term is used in ancient Greece to describe a form of government that puts power in the hands of a small elite. Literally it means 'the rule of the best'. Aristotle regarded it as superior to oligarchy (below) because it confers benefits on the basis of merit and values all persons' interests. It gives power to those who most deserve to govern and is therefore preferable to monarchy, democracy and polity, which he says are concerned only with matters of wealth.

Authoritarianism A form of oppressive government with strong centralized power and limited political freedoms or competing institutions such as legislatures or political parties.

Communitarianism The theory that it is not the individual or the state or any other entity but the community that ought to be the focus of our values and legal and political analysis. See 'individualism'.

Consequentialism The belief that whether an act is morally right depends exclusively on its consequences or on some quality related to the act, e.g., the motive behind it or the existence of a general rule requiring acts of the same kind.

Conservatism A political doctrine that emphasizes the value of traditional institutions and practices – that it seeks to conserve.

Contractarianism The view that since people are largely selfish, to maximize their self-interest they are most likely to adopt the right moral choices under a hypothetical social contract that assumes when they are, in Rawls's model, in the 'original position (below), they will rationally agree to certain terms and, in particular, to the authority of the government.

Democracy A system of government in which all are involved in making decisions about the affairs of the state, normally by voting to elect representatives to a parliament or similar body. It is generally conceived as government 'by the people' or, at least, by the majority.

Deontological The view that certain acts are intrinsically right or wrong, regardless of their consequences. It means 'duty-based'. See also 'consequentialism'.

Difference Principle The second part of the second principle of John Rawls's theory of justice. The first principle requires that citizens enjoy equal basic liberties. The first part of the second principle requires fair equality of opportunity, which has priority over the difference principle. The difference principle governs the distribution of income and wealth, positions of responsibility and power and the social bases of self-respect. It holds that inequalities in the distribution of these goods are accepted only if they benefit the least well-off members of society.

Egalitarianism A theory that is generally based on the idea that all people are fundamentally equal and should be treated as equals and enjoy an equality of social status.

Free market A system in which prices are governed by the open market and the operation of supply and demand with little or no interference by the government.

Incommensurability The idea that moral dilemmas are incapable of resolution since they cannot be measured against a common standard. How, for instance, is one to measure 'truth' against 'love'? Compare with 'utilitarianism' (which avoids this problem by claiming that all values may be reduced to one: happiness).

Individualism The theory that individuals be accorded primary moral importance and, as Kant argued, must be regarded as ends in themselves with autonomy and inviolable rights. Compare with 'communitarianism'. See also 'Kantianism'.

Kantianism In ethics, the thesis that moral judgements are expressions of practical, rather than theoretical, reason. Practical reason, according to Kant, is derived from its own rational nature. The 'autonomy of the will' is the capacity to use practical reason to produce standards of conduct and constitutes the basis of human dignity. This will is autonomous only if the principles it generates are capable of being universal laws and so create 'categorical imperatives', i.e., unconditionally binding duties. Importantly, Kant insists that people are ends in themselves and must not be used instrumentally as utilitarianism appears to do. Compare with 'utilitarianism'.

Liberalism A political philosophy that, in very broad terms, embraces liberty (below), equality and the traditional democratic freedoms including free speech, freedom of religion, tolerance, civil liberties and the free market.

Libertarianism A political philosophy that stresses the importance of liberty (below), individual autonomy and freedom of choice. It is opposed to the power and intrusion of the government in the lives of citizens and generally advocates laissez faire capitalism and rights to private property.

Liberty The idea that comprises those freedoms to which all members of society are entitled, unless they encroach on the freedom of others; implies the absence of arbitrary limitations on personal freedom.

Maximin rule Dictates that when making a choice, we play safe by choosing the alternative whose worst outcome leaves us better off than the worst outcome of all other alternatives. Rawls argues that the people in the original position would rationally opt for this strategy when choosing among the principles of justice. It results in their selecting the principles of justice over the principles of utility because, unlike utilitarianism, justice as fairness ensures equal basic liberties, fair equal opportunities and an adequate social minimum for everyone.

Oligarchy A form of rule in which power is in the hands of a small number of individuals who might be members of a particular family, corporation or military, religious, royal or other grouping. Aristotle uses the term (literally 'the rule of the few') to describe a government controlled by a minority consisting of the wealthy. Unlike aristocracy, Aristotle regards it as an immoral form of government because the ruling faction governs solely in its own interests, disregarding those of the poor.

Original position An imaginary condition, described by Rawls, in which the 'people in the original position' (the POP) choose principles to determine the basic structure of the society they will inhabit. To ensure rationality and impartiality, they decide behind a 'veil of ignorance', behind which they are stripped of knowledge about their gender, race, social position and conception of what constitutes a good life.

Polis Generally translated to mean 'city'. In Greece it was a fairly small, autonomous region governed by an elite class of citizens. The workforce comprised slaves, manual labourers and women. Aristotle's world consisted of several city-states and his philosophy is based on the assumption that the *polis* is the most practical form of government.

Polity An organized, institutionalized political unit composed of a group of people united by a cohesive force such as their identity.

Postmodernism A broad multi-disciplinary assault on the values of the Enlightenment, especially the idea of objective human knowledge achieved through reason in pursuit of universal objective truths.

Pragmatism The theory that attempts to explain meaning and truth in terms of the application of ideas or beliefs to the performance of actions that have practical or effective outcomes.

Prioritarianism The view that the quality of an outcome depends on satisfaction of the general welfare of people, with extra consideration given to the worst-off.

Priority of the right over the good The idea that what accords with duty (see 'deontological') should trump what produces the best consequences (see 'utilitarianism').

Reflective equilibrium A process described by Rawls as involving what he calls our shared 'considered convictions' of justice from the particular to the general. It then attempts to determine the principles of justice that best 'fit' with these considered convictions in a 'wide reflective equilibrium' after deliberating on all the reasonable alternative conceptions of justice.

Relativism The general view that our judgements are conditioned by the specific social context of a particular individual, time or place. Ethical relativism denies the existence of universal standards of moral value and claims that moral judgements depend on the cultural norms of particular societies.

Social contractarianism See 'Contractarianism'.

Subjectivism Regards moral judgement as depending on the arbitrary, personal or individual, rather than rational, objective standards.

Totalitarianism A repressive political system with unlimited state power that attempts to control every aspect of the lives of citizens by propaganda, strict regulation of the economy, civil liberties, surveillance and terror.

Tyranny An autocratic form of rule in which one individual exercises power without legal restraint; implies the illegitimate possession or use of such power. Aristotle describes it as a form of monarchy that has diverged from the ideal; a tyrant is a violent usurper.

Utilitarianism The approach to morality that regards pleasure or the satisfaction of desire as the exclusive element in human good and treats the morality of acts and rules as wholly dependent on the consequences for human welfare. See 'consequentialism'.

Notes and further reading

The references and readings are, in general, confined to sources that are both introductory and accessible. I have (with a few exceptions) avoided academic articles and stuck to books. Their date of publication does not necessarily reflect when they first appeared; I have tried to refer to editions that are easily available.

Readers new to philosophy will find an invaluable guide in Peter Cave whose *Philosophy: A Beginner's Guide* (Oneworld, 2011) is an outstanding vade mecum to the subject. I also recommend his excellent *Ethics* (2015) in the same series. Also helpful is Edward Craig's *Philosophy: A Very Short Introduction* (OUP, 2002) and Peter Singer's *Practical Ethics* (CUP, 3rd edn, 2011). Stanford University's invaluable online *Encyclopaedia of Philosophy* can be read with profit on almost every conceivable aspect of the subject and I have both learnt from it and drawn upon it in a number of places in this book. For an introduction to the specific subject of theories of justice, look no further than Michael Sandel's justly popular *Justice: What's the Right Thing to Do?* (Penguin, 2009).

In the unfortunate contest between non-sexist pronouns and non-cumbersome expression, the latter has generally prevailed in this book. I hope this is not unjust.

Chapter 1: Justice and injustice

The erstwhile system of apartheid in South Africa continues to attract academic attention. A recent penetrating account is Saul Dubow's *Apartheid 1948–1994* (OUP, 2014). Nelson Mandela's autobiography, *Long Walk to Freedom* (Abacus, 1995), is more than a political analysis; it provides an inspiring insight to the life of this legendary leader. Comparisons are often drawn between the system of apartheid and the evils of Hitler's German Reich, brilliantly examined in William L. Shirer's magisterial, *The Rise and Fall of the Third Reich* (Arrow, 1991), amongst many other works.

Text box: Right and wrong

The quotation from Joseph Conrad is from his classic, *Heart of Darkness.* Burke's aphorism is from his *Reflections on the Revolution in France.*

Chapter 2: Justice and virtue

The complete works of Aristotle (running to more than 8,000 pages) are available for download to your Kindle for the princely sum of £1.49. No, I don't understand it either. A short and sweet secondary source is Jonathan Barnes, *Aristotle: A Very Short Introduction* (OUP, 2000). Roger Scruton has written a useful introduction to Kant's moral philosophy in the same series.

In *The Concept of Law*, H.L.A. Hart argues that the idea of justice consists of two parts: a uniform or constant feature, summarized in the precept 'Treat like cases alike' and a shifting or varying criterion used in determining when, for any given purpose, cases are alike or different. He suggests that today the principle that, prima facie, human beings are entitled to be treated alike has become so extensively recognized that racial discrimination is usually defended on the ground that those discriminated against are not 'fully human'. The Roman approach to justice is to be found in the *Corpus Juris Civilis* (the body of law codified under the order of the Emperor Justinian) where it is described as 'the constant and perpetual wish to give everyone that which they deserve'. It adds that 'the precepts of the law are … to live honestly, not to injure others and to grant everyone his due'. But what is a person's due? This is left uncertain, although the statement, albeit rather broad, does capture the central overlapping features of a reasonable conception of justice: the importance of the individual, that people are treated consistently, impartially and equally.

The quotation from Aristotle about the *polis* is from *The Politics*, Book III, Chapter ix. The longer quote is from the same work, Book III, Chapter xii. His reference to 'moral excellence' is from *Nichomachean Ethics*, Book II, Chapter 1.

Chapter 3: Rights, dignity and freedom

My (inexcusable) cryptic reference to Woody Allen springs from the fact that his real name is Allan Konigsberg, the same as Kant's hometown. Kant's statements concerning suicide are from his *The Metaphysics of Morals*. The quote about lying comes from 'On a Supposed Right to Lie' and his unyielding declaration about capital punishment is from *Introduction to the Metaphysics of Morals.* The quotation from Hume is from his *Treatise concerning Human Nature* (Book II, Part III, Sec. III, p. 415). The quotations from James Griffin are from his book *On Human Rights* (OUP, 2008), 14–15, 198.

Text box: The International Bill of Human Rights

The quotation is from the International Bill of Rights Fact Sheet 2: http://www.ohchr.org/Documents/Publications/FactSheet2Rev.1en.pdf

Chapter 4: Utilitarianism

Hart's point is made in his *Essays on Bentham* (Clarendon Press, 1982), 4. Mill's reference to Bentham's 'battering-ram' is quoted by Gerald J. Postema, *Bentham and the Common Law Tradition* (Clarendon Press, 1986), 148. J.J.C. Smart's reference to 'hedonistic' utilitarianism is from the outstanding book, J.J.C. Smart and Bernard Williams' *Utilitarianism: For and Against* (CUP, 1973). The famous passage from Bentham is taken from his *An Introduction to the Principles of Morals and Legislation*, Chapter 1, para 1. My Linda example is adapted from Nigel Simmonds, *Central Issues in Jurisprudence*, 4th edn (Sweet & Maxwell, 2014), 26.

Text box: Utilitarian dilemmas

The trolley hypothesis belongs to the philosopher Philippa Foot (1920–2010). The fat man twist is suggested by Judith Jarvis Thomson. Jim in the jungle is the invention of Sir Bernard Williams.

The quotation that begins 'It is proper to state …' is from J.S. Mill's *On Liberty* and may be found in Chapter 1.11. The italics are mine. The sentence beginning 'He who does anything …' is from *On Liberty*, Chapter 3, and that which starts 'Of two pleasures …' is from *On Liberty,* Chapter 2. The extract from H.L.A. Hart is from his essay 'Between Utility and Rights' in his *Essays in Jurisprudence and Philosophy* (Clarendon Press, 1983). The statement by Williams 'No one can hold …' is from Smart and Williams, *Utilitarianism: For and Against*, 82. The reference to 'regress' is in Smart and Williams, *Utilitarianism: For and Against*, 82. The defence of utilitarianism against the 'separateness of persons' element is cogently pleaded by Richard Chappell: http://www.philosophyetc.net/2012/02/separateness-of-persons.html

Chapter 5: Justice as fairness

The quotation from Hobbes is from Chapter 13 of *Leviathan*. Rousseau's statement appears in his *Social Contract*, Vol IV. Compare Ronald Dworkin, *Justice for Hedgehogs* (Harvard University Press, 2011), 63–5, 267–9. See also Thomas Pogge, *John Rawls: His Life and Theory of Justice*, translated by M. Kosch (OUP, 2007). Rawls's description of the social contract appears on page 12 of *A Theory of Justice* (OUP, 2002). The next quotes are from pages 20 and 48–51 respectively. The italics are mine. His account of the 'maximin' principle is from page 287. Modifications to his original position appear in *Political Liberalism* (Columbia University Press, 1993) and *The Law of Peoples* (Harvard University Press, 1999). The sentence beginning '[A]n initial acquiescence …' is on page 168 of *Political Liberalism*. The quotations on the 'just savings principle' are from *A Theory of Justice* page 252 and 289 respectively.

Text box: Rawls: critics' compliments

The quotation from Nozick is from his *Anarchy, State and Utopia* (Wiley-Blackwell, 2001), 183. Dworkin's tribute is from *Justice in Robes* (Harvard University Press, 2006), 34, 261.

The various criticisms of Rawls are from 'The Original Position' in Daniels (ed.), *Reading Rawls*, 16. H.L.A. Hart, 'Rawls on Liberty and its Priority' in both his *Essays in Jurisprudence and Philosophy*, 223, and Daniels (ed.), *Reading Rawls*, (Harvard University Press,1989), 230; T.M. Scanlon, *What We Owe Each Other* (Harvard University Press, 2000); M. Fisk, 'History and Reason in Rawls' Moral Theory' in N. Daniels (ed), *Reading Rawls,* 53; R. Miller, 'Rawls and Marxism' in the same collection, 206; Martha C. Nussbaum, *Frontiers of Justice: Disability, Nationality, Species Membership* (Belknap Press, 2006). The feminist critique mounted by Carole Pateman is from *The Sexual Contract* (Stanford University Press, 1988). Susan Moller Okin's book is *Justice, Gender and the Family* (Basic Books, 1989). The communitarian analysis is represented by Michael Sandel, *Liberalism and the Limits of Justice* (Cambridge University Press, 1982); Charles Taylor, 'Atomism' in his *Philosophical Papers*, vol. 2, 210, quoted in Steven Lukes, *Moral Conflict and Politics* (Clarendon Press, 1991), 73. The 'stripped' quote from Sandel is on page 178 of *Liberalism and the Limits of Justice.* Bentham's pronouncement comes from *An Introduction to the Principles of Morals and Legislation*, 38–39. The quotation about 'moral desert' is on page 313. The long extract starting '[A]n initial acquiescence …' is from *Political Liberalism*, 168. My concluding quotation is taken from *A Theory of Justice*, 587. A slightly different approach to social justice comes from David Miller who, in *Principles of Social Justice* (Harvard University Press, 2001) advances a theory of justice based on need, desert and equality.

Chapter 6: Libertarianism

The influence of Hayek on Nozick's theory is plain; in *The Road to Serfdom*, for example, Hayek says: 'Strictly speaking, there is no "economic motive" but only economic factors conditioning our striving for other ends. What in ordinary language is misleadingly called the "economic motive" means merely the desire for general opportunity, the desire for power to achieve unspecified ends. If we strive for money, it is because it offers us the widest choice in enjoying the fruits of our labor', Friedrich von Hayek, *The Road to Serfdom* (Routledge & Kegan Paul, 1986, 98). Among his other important works is *The Constitution of Liberty* (Routledge & Kegan Paul, reprinted 1963). A good reader on Nozick is Geoffrey Paul (ed.), *Reading Nozick: Essays on* Anarchy, State and Utopia (Basil Blackwell, 1981). For a penetrating critique of

Nozick's perspective, see Robert Wolff, *Robert Nozick: Property, Justice and the Minimal State* (Polity Press, 1991).

Ayn Rand's novels, especially *The Fountainhead* and *Atlas Shrugged*, were enormously successful. She expounds a theory that she calls 'objectivism', which regards man as an heroic being whose noblest moral purpose is to secure his own happiness and whose noblest activity is his productive achievement.

The quotation 'Seizing …' is from Nozick's *Anarchy, State and Utopia* (Basil Blackwell, 1974), 172. The reference to holdings occurs on page 153; the quotation 'there is no moral …' is on page 33; the reference to Mars is on page 174. The quote from H.L.A. Hart is from his essay 'Between Utility and Rights' in *Essays in Jurisprudence and Philosophy*, 205.

The extracts are from John Clare's poem 'The Moors' (or 'Mores'). Have a look as well at his moving poem on this subject, 'To a Fallen Elm'. A fine account of this extraordinary poet's life and work is Jonathan Bate, *John Clare: A Biography* (Picador, 2004). This poem, along with many more, is to be found in the same author's *Selected Poetry of John Clare* (Faber, 2004).

Chapter 7: Capability

The most accessible accounts of the theory are Amartya Sen, *The Idea of Justice* (Penguin, 2010) and Martha Nussbaum, *Creating Capabilities: The Human Development Approach* (Harvard University Press, 2013). The disabled person example is from Sen, 306–7. The quotation is from page 307. Nussbaum's list is from *Frontiers of Justice: Disability, Nationality, Species Membership* (Harvard University Press, 2006), 76–78. John Finnis's list is from *Natural Law and Natural Rights,* 2nd edn (OUP, 2011).

The capability approach has been adopted by numerous writers on human development such as Sakiko Fukuda-Parr. Sen's followers, in addition to Nussbaum, include Ingrid Robeyns, (development ethics), Sabina Alkire (an alternative to social cost-benefit analysis), Wolff and de-Shalit (policy approaches to welfare state design). The literature is large and expanding: Sakiko Fukuda-Parr and A.K. Shiva Kumar, *Handbook of Human Development: Concepts, Measures and Policies* (OUP, 2009); David Clark, *Visions of Development: A Study of Human Values* (Edward Elgar, 2002); Ingrid Robeyns, *The Capability Approach* (Open Book, 2014); Sabina Alkire, *Valuing Freedoms: Sen's Capability Approach and Poverty Reduction* (OUP, 2002); Jonathan Wolff and Avner de-Shalit, *Disadvantage* (OUP, 2007); Christopher A. Riddle, *Disability and Justice: The Capabilities Approach in Practice* (Lexington Books/Rowman & Littlefield, 2014).

Chapter 8: Justice and the free market

The classic defence of free market economics is Milton Friedman's *Capitalism and Freedom*, 40th anniversary edition (University of Chicago Press, 2002). Two handy introductions to this topic are Partha Dasgupta, *Economics* (2007) and James Fulcher *Capitalism* (2nd edn, 2015) both published by OUP in their Very Short Introduction series.

Text box: The Coase theorem

The example is adapted from A.M. Polinsky, *An Introduction to Law and Economics* (Little, Brown, 1983).

The Baby M case is discussed in *Justice* 91 ff. The case is reported as *In re Baby M*, 217 New Jersey Superior Court 313 (1987) and *Matter of Baby M*, Supreme Court of New Jersey, 537 *Atlantic Reporter*, 2nd Series, 1227 (1988). The reference to 'marketizing' appears in *Justice*, 265.

Chapter 9: Equality

The quotation from Rawls is from *A Theory of Justice*, 510. Ronald Dworkin's statement is from his chapter 'Why Liberals Should Care about Equality' in *A Matter of Principle* (Harvard University Press, 1985), 205. The longer quote is from *Sovereign Virtue: The Theory and Practice of Equality* (Harvard University Press, 2000) 287. His observation about liberty and equality is from *Justice for Hedgehogs* (Harvard University Press, 2011), 331. Amartya Sen's criticism of Dworkin is on page 265 of *The Idea of Justice*. Another leading critic of equality is Larry Temkin whose analysis of the concept is to be found in his book, *Inequality* (Oxford University Press, 1993). For a biting satire of how social equality can result in a frightening levelling down of everyone, see Kurt Vonnegut's famous science-fiction short story 'Harrison Bergeron'.

Text box: Votes for women

Source: https://en.wikipedia.org/wiki/Women%27s_suffrage, where a more detailed list may be found.

Text box: Race and criminal justice

Sources: US Department of Justice, Bureau of Justice Statistics, September 2015. www.bjs.gov/content/pub/pdf/p14.pdf; Marc Mauer and David Cole. 'Five Myths about Americans in Prison' *Washington Post*, 17 June 2011.

Chapter 10: Fraternity

The extract from Luce Irigaray is taken from *Thinking the Difference: For A Peaceful Revolution*, translated by K. Montin (Athlone Press, 1994), 59. Catharine MacKinnon's charge is from 'Feminism, Marxism, Method and the State: Toward Feminist Jurisprudence'

(1983) 8, *Signs: Journal of Women, Culture & Society,* 63. See also Martha Nussbaum, *Sex and Social Justice* (OUP, 2000). The quotation is from *Frontiers of Justice: Disability, Nationality, Species Membership* (Belknap Press, 2006), 103. Susan Moller Okin's book is *Justice, Gender and the Family* (Basic Books, 1991). My quotation from Iris Marion Young is taken from her *Justice and the Politics of Difference* (Princeton University Press, 2011), 242. MacKinnon's words are from her *Feminism Unmodified* (Harvard University Press, 1987), 173. The quote from Rawls appears on page 512 of *A Theory of Justice.*

Text box: Gender at work

Source: The World Bank, *Gender at Work: A Companion to the World Development Report on Jobs*, 2013. http://www.worldbank.org/en/topic/gender/publication/gender-at-work-companion-report-to-world-development-report-2013-jobs

Text box: Compassion towards animals

See J.M. Coetzee's novel, *The Lives of Animals* (Profile Books, 2000).

The quotation from Bernard E. Rollin is taken from his *The Unheeded Cry: Animal Consciousness, Animal Pain and Science* (OUP, 1989); Stephen R.L. Clark: *The Moral Status of Animals*, (OUP, 1977) 141–2.

Bentham's famous expression of compassion for animals is from his *An Introduction to the Principles of Morals and Legislation* (Dover, 2007). See too Cass R. Sunstein and Martha C. Nussbaum (eds.), *Animal Rights: Current Debates and New Directions* (OUP, 2004). The starting point for any account of this subject is Peter Singer's trail-blazing *Animal Liberation*, which appeared almost twenty years ago; a new edition was published in 2015 by Bodley Head. See also his *Practical Ethics* (CUP, 1979). A first-rate introduction to the subject of animal rights is David de Grazia, *Animal Rights: A Very Short Introduction* (OUP, 2002).

The quotation from Kant comes from his *Lectures on Ethics*, translated and edited by P. Heath and J.B. Schneewind (CUP, 1997), 212 (27: 459). I recommend Thomas Scanlon's admirable *What We Owe to Each Other* (Belknap, 1998). The Nussbaum quote is from her *Frontiers of Justice: Disability, Nationality, Species Membership*, 351. The passage of Tom Regan's comes from his fine book, *The Case for Animal Rights* (University of California Press, 2004), 397.

The Indian case *Nair* v *Union of India* (2000). Kerala High Court No 155/1999 is cited by Nussbaum, in *Frontiers of Justice*, page 325. Catharine MacKinnon's comment is from her essay 'Of Mice and Men: A Feminist Fragment on Animal Rights' in Cass R. Sunstein and Martha C. Nussbaum (eds.), *Animal Rights: Current Debates and New Directions* (OUP, 2004), 271.

Chapter 11: Communitarianism

Michael Sandel's comment appears at the beginning of his communitarian treatise, *Liberalism and the Limits of Justice* (CUP, 1982), 1. The quotations from Alisdair MacIntyre are from his *After Virtue*, 3rd edn. (Duckworth, 985), 204–5; 220. Charles Taylor's remarks are taken from his essay 'Atomism' in his *Philosophical Papers*, vol. 2, 210, quoted in Steven Lukes, *Moral Conflict and Politics* (Clarendon Press, 1991), 73. The quotation from Albert H.Y. Chen is from his chapter 'Human Rights in China' in Raymond Wacks (ed.), *Human Rights in Hong Kong* (OUP, 1992), 178.

Text box: Female genital mutilation

The 2016 report by the World Health Organization *Female Genital Mutilation* may be found at http://www.who.int/mediacentre/factsheets/fs241/en/

The statistics for England are published by the Health and Social Care Information Centre (HSCIC) whose report is available at http://www.hscic.gov.uk/article/7180/First-ever-annual-statistical-publication-for-FGM-shows-5700-newly-recorded-cases-during-2015-16

A harrowing account of the practice – from the victims' point of view – is described by Aayan Hirsi Ali in her remarkable book *Infidel* (Simon & Schuster, 2008).

Chapter 12: Global justice

The principal works I have drawn on here are Thomas Pogge, *World Poverty and Human Rights: Cosmopolitan Responsibilities and Reforms* (Polity, 2002); Charles Beitz, *Political Theory and International Relations* (Princeton University Press, 1979); Michael Walzer, *Spheres of Justice*, (Basic Books, 1983); Bruce Ackerman, *Social Justice in the Liberal State* (Yale University Press, 1980). The quotation appears on page 95.

The source of these statistics is the 2012 United Nations *Millennium Development Goals Report* where you will find an enormous quantity of information. It may be found at http://www.un.org/millenniumgoals/pdf/MDG%20Report%202012.pdf. The data on life expectancy is from *Global Health Observatory Data Repository: Life Expectancy – Data by Country (CSV). Geneva, Switzerland: World Health Statistics 2015, World Health Organization, relating to the year 2013*. The *Millennium Development Goals* may be discovered at http://www.un.org/millenniumgoals/bkgd.shtml. The statistics on children are from http://www.un.org/sustainabledevelopment/blog/2016/06/unicef-report-growing-inequalities-threaten-most-disadvantaged-kids/

The Sustainable Development Goals are set out in paragraph 54 United Nations Resolution A/RES/70/1 of 25 September 2015.

See http://www.un.org/ga/search/view_doc.asp?symbol=A/RES/70/1&Lang=E

Text box: Access to education

Source: http://www.unicef.org/education/bege_61657.html

Chapter 13: Achieving social justice

The statistics on modern slavery are from 'Where the World's Slaves Live' *The Atlantic* http://www.theatlantic.com/news/archive/2016/05/where-the-worlds-slaves-live/484994/ and the International Labour Organization's report http://www.ilo.org/global/topics/forced-labour/lang--en/index.htm

The encouraging news is reported by the United Nations *Millennium Development Goals Report 2012* to be found at http://www.un.org/millenniumgoals/poverty.shtml

The World Health Organization's statistics on undernourishment and child mortality were produced by its Global Health Observatory and can be found here: http://www.who.int/gho/child_health/mortality/mortality_under_five_text/en/

The World Bank's 2016 report, *Country and Lending Groups* https://datahelpdesk.worldbank.org/knowledgebase/articles/906519

The figures of life expectancy are from the *United Nations World Population Prospects 2012 Revision*: https://esa.un.org/unpd/wpp/publications/Files/WPP2012_HIGHLIGHTS.pdf

The other encouraging statistics are from Johan Norberg, *Progress: Ten Reasons to Look Forward to the Future* (Oneworld, 2016).

The flute parable is from Amartya Sen's *The Idea of Justice,* 12–15.

My gloomy impression of post-apartheid South Africa has been slightly brightened thanks to my dialogues with the distinguished former judge of the Constitutional Court, Justice Albie Sachs, who, inter alia, reminded me of the significance of the African concept of 'ubuntu' (sometimes translated as 'human kindness' or 'humaneness') in the quest for justice in that troubled land. He describes it as encompassing individualism and communitarianism, yet elastic enough to cover many social and policy formations. His own contribution to the cause of justice is widely acknowledged; see, for example, Drucilla Cornell and Karen van Marle, *Albie Sachs and Transformation in South Africa: From Revolutionary Activist to Constitutional Court Judge* (Routledge, 2015). For a fuller account of 'ubuntu' see https://en.wikipedia.org/wiki/Ubuntu_%28philosophy%29

After the dismantling of the apartheid system, a Truth and Reconciliation Commission was established. It provided the opportunity for anyone who believed they had been a victim of violence or injustice to be heard by this judicial-like forum. Those who had committed acts of violence could also give evidence and seek amnesty from prosecution. Several sessions of its proceedings were broadcast on national television. The process, despite its shortcomings, is generally regarded as an important element in the transition toward democracy.

Text box: Religious persecution

Source: The United States Commission on International Religious Freedom (USCIRF) Annual Report 2016 http://www.uscirf.gov/

Index

abortion 165
Ackerman, Bruce 171
act utilitarianism 35
Afghanistan 170
Africa 157, 159, 177; *see also* South Africa
African-Americans 116
After Virtue (MacIntyre) 148
altruism 39, 167
anarchism 76
Anarchy, State and Utopia (Nozick) 72
Animal Liberation (Singer) 138
animal rights 38, 68, 134–44, 145–6, 156
anti-egalitarianism 108–11
anti-trust laws 99, 103
apartheid 1–5, 27, 30, 61, 186
aristocracy 188
Aristotle 8, 10–11, 12–17, 18–20, 149
  and animals 136
  and Aquinas 86
  and equality 107
Asian values 153–4
asylum seekers 159
authoritarianism 52, 188

bear farming 144
Beitz, Charles 164, 176
Bentham, Jeremy 14, 33–5, 38, 41, 42–3, 44
  and animals 139
Berlin, Isaiah 26
border control 170–2
Brown v Board of Education of Topeka (1954) 105
brute luck 115–16, 130–1
Burke, Edmund 8

capability 82–6, 87–94, 113, 119, 165–9
  and animals 139–40
  and disability 131, 134
capitalism 9, 50, 62, 97, 99
Carlyle, Thomas 41
Case for Animal Rights, The (Regan) 142
caste system 181
categorical imperative 23–4, 31–2
character 14
Chen, Albert H.Y. 153
Chicago School 96
children 6, 15, 122, 141, 154
  and education 159
  and mortality rates 180–1
citizenship 14–15
civil disobedience 61
civil rights movement 61
civil society 72, 147
Clare, John 80
Clark, Stephen R.L. 139
class 17, 66
climate change 156, 158, 173–4
Coase theorem 99, 100
Cohen, G.A. 119–20
colonialism 78
command economy 97
communism 97
communitarianism 30, 51, 52, 113–14, 147–8, 149–55
  and definition 188
  and free market 99
  and Rawls 63, 64, 66–7
compassion 89, 139, 140
compensation 78, 79, 98, 115
competition 77
Confucianism 153, 154
Conrad, Joseph 8

conscription 102
consequentialism 14, 18, 35–6, 41, 42–3, 188
conservatism 117, 188
constitutionalism 14–16, 62
contractarianism, *see* social contract
Convention on the Elimination of All Forms of Discrimination 121
conversion factors 90–1
corrective justice 12–13
corruption 156, 157, 163
crimes against humanity 3, 176
Crito (Plato) 46
culture 30, 151, 170–1, 175

Da Vinci, Leonardo 139
Dante Alighieri 174
De Jure Belli ac Pacis (Grotius) 166
deafness 132–4
democracy 15, 16–17, 52, 154, 186, 189
  and Rawls 62, 63–4, 149
deontology 14, 18, 21, 22, 189
Descartes, René 136
deserts 8, 59, 68, 71
despotism 15
detachment 54–5
dictatorships 156
difference feminism 125–6, 128
difference principle 57–9, 64, 66, 67–8, 69–70, 113
  and definition 189
  and global justice 161
  and Nozick 78
dignity 24, 84, 87, 92, 119, 166
disability 68, 83–4, 90, 108, 115–16, 129–34
  and discrimination 145
discrimination 1–6, 12, 61, 62, 104, 105
  and the disabled 132, 145
  and women 121–3
disease 6, 157–8, 169
distributive justice 13, 44, 72, 75–6, 164
domestic violence 122, 124, 127
duty 14, 21, 23, 24
Dworkin, Andrea 129
Dworkin, Ronald 12, 57, 65–6, 119–20, 130–1
  and equality 112, 114–15, 117–19

education 62, 104, 105, 147, 159
  and global justice 168, 169
egalitarianism, *see* equality
employment 62, 104, 122, 123, 161; *see also* unemployment
enclosure movement 80
energy 173
Engels, Friedrich 97
English Civil War 47
entitlement theory 71–2, 74–5, 80, 81
environment, the 156, 158, 168, 169, 173–4
equality 48, 104–5, 107–8, 111–15, 119–20, 183
  and animals 138
  and Aristotle 10–13, 15, 20
  and definition 189
  and the disabled 131–2
  and freedom 117–19
  and Rawls 57–8, 59, 62, 64
  and Rousseau 51, 52–3
  and women 123–4, 126
  see also anti-egalitarianism; inequality
ethics 13–14, 99, 140, 143–4
Europe 170
external preferences 112

fairness 46, 54, 167
family 126–7, 128, 147, 148, 169
female genital mutilation (FGM) 122, 151, 152
feminism 67, 111, 123–9, 134, 143, 145
Finnis, John 86–7
formal equality 105
free market 12, 95–103, 118–20, 160–1, 189
freedom, *see* liberty
freedom of movement 2, 27, 170, 171, 172
freedom of speech 40–1, 167
French Revolution 50
Friedman, Milton 96
functionings 87–91

Gandhi, Mahatma 61
gender 91, 92, 122; *see also* men; women
general will 51–3
genocide 65, 156, 176

Gilligan, Carol 126
global justice 6, 160–2, 163–9, 176–8
global warming 173–4
globalization 156, 160–1
government 47, 48–9, 50, 51, 52–3
  and equality 104, 105, 110, 114–15, 117–18
  and free market 96, 99
  and global justice 162, 163, 174–6
  and Nozick 72, 73–4, 76–7, 79–80
greenhouse gases 173–4
Griffin, James 29
Gross Domestic Product (GDP) 91, 168
Grotius, Hugo 165–6
Groundwork for the Metaphysics of Morals (Kant) 22

happiness 24, 33, 38–40, 41, 45
  and Bentham 34–5, 42
Hart, H.L.A. 42, 79
Hayek, F.A. von 72, 96
health care 62, 104, 157
Hegel, Georg Wilhelm Friedrich 150
Heraclitus 8
Hicks, John 98
historical injustice 78, 80
Hobbes, Thomas 47–9, 127–8, 174
Holocaust, the 26, 30
homosexuality 179
Human Development Index (HDI) 91
human rights 24, 25–8, 29–30, 65, 154–5, 156
  and communitarianism 150–1
  and women 121
humanitarianism 169, 170
Hume, David 31

immigration 162, 170–2
In a Different Voice (Gilligan) 126
incommensurability 189–90
India 61, 181
individualism 10, 30, 66, 125, 150, 190
inequality 5–7, 55, 110–11, 161, 162–3, 183
  and gender 91, 92
injustice 1–5, 82, 156–8
institutions 167–8, 185
International Bill of Human Rights (1976) 27
International Borrowing and Resource Privileges 163
International Criminal Court (ICC) 3, 176–8
international governmental organizations (IGOs) 175
International Labour Organization (ILO) 175
intolerance 179
Iraq 170
Irigary, Luce 125–6
Islam 122, 152, 170–1, 172

Jefferson, Thomas 50
Johnson, Samuel 8
jury system 55
just savings principle 59–60
Justice for Hedgehogs (Dworkin) 117

Kaldor, Nicholas 98
Kant, Immanuel 14, 21–6, 30–1, 32, 36, 45
  and animals 136, 137
  and global justice 174–5, 176
  and Nozick 72
  and rights 148–9
  and Rousseau 53
  and women 129
Kantianism 190
Keynes, John Maynard 97
King, Martin Luther, Jr 61

Law of Peoples, The (Rawls) 64–5, 149, 161, 162, 176
League of Nations 175
Leviathan (Hobbes) 47
LGBT community 179
liberalism 63, 64–5, 123–4, 127, 151, 190
libertarianism 8, 12, 71–81, 190
liberty 12, 26, 83–4, 183, 190
  and equality 117–19
  and Kant 21, 24
  and Mill 40–1
  and Rawls 57, 59, 66
  and Rousseau 52–3
life expectancy 157, 180–1

Locke, John 49–50, 128, 136
  and Nozick 72, 73, 76, 80
lying 22, 30, 31–2

MacIntyre, Alasdair 148, 149
MacKinnon, Catharine 124–5, 129, 143
malevolence 44
Malthus, Thomas 96
Mandela, Nelson 4, 8
market, the 71, 72, 77, 153–4; *see also* free market
Marx, Karl 41, 97
Marxism 66, 99
maximin principle 58–9, 191
men 124–6, 129
migration 156, 159, 162, 170–2
military, the 102, 156
Mill, John Stuart 34, 38–41, 43–4, 97
Millennium Development Goals (MDGs) 158
minimal state 77, 79–80
Montesquieu 8
morality 13, 18, 34, 39, 43, 48
  and animals 135–9, 141, 143–4
  and communitarianism 150, 152
  and equality 105, 108, 110–11
  and Kant 22, 23–6, 30–1
mortality rates 180–1
motivation 23–4, 31, 35, 39, 43
multi-nationals 160, 162, 168

Nagel, Thomas 164
Nair v Union of India (2000) 141
'nanny state' 74
nation-states 160
nationalism 163, 164
natural resources 156–7, 164–5
nature state 49–50, 86
Nicomachean Ethics (Aristotle) 10
North Atlantic Treaty Organization (NATO) 175
Nozick, Robert 46, 57, 67, 71–81, 95, 108
  and animals 135, 136
Nuremberg Trials 177
Nussbaum, Martha 68, 82, 84–6, 89, 92, 184
  and animals 139–40
  and disability 131
  and global justice 161–2, 165–8

Occupy movement 6–7
Okin, Susan Moller 126–7
oligarchy 15, 16, 17, 191
On Liberty (Mill) 38, 40
opportunity 107, 109, 117, 118
oppression 30, 65, 128, 151
original position 55–7, 58–60, 61–2, 65, 66, 184
  and definition 191
  and disability 129–30
overlapping consensus 63–4

pain 34–5, 39, 44, 138, 144
Pareto, Vilfredo 97–8
Parfit, Derek 108–9
Pateman, Carol 67, 128
paternalism 15, 92
patriarchy 67, 124, 125, 128
peace 48
Peace of Westphalia (1648) 160
Plato 10, 30, 143–4
pleasure 34–5, 38–9, 42, 43–4, 138
Pogge, Thomas 162–3, 164, 176
polis (city-state) 16, 19, 86, 191
Political Liberalism (Rawls) 63, 149
politics 2, 10, 13, 62, 63–5, 117
  and Aristotle 14–16, 19–20
  see also government
Politics (Aristotle) 10
polity 16, 191
POP (people in the original position) 55–7, 58–60, 61–2, 66, 68, 129–30
population growth 156–7
pornography 125, 126, 129
postmodernism 192
poverty 5, 6–7, 17, 108–9, 117
  and decline 181–2
  and equality 115
  and free market 96–7
  and global 157–8, 160–1, 162–3, 168–9
  and Rawls 67–8
pragmatism 192
preferences 36, 45, 112–13
prioritarianism 108–9, 192

private sector 72
private will 52
promises 36
property rights 49–50, 71, 73, 78, 80
proportional equality 107
prostitution 67, 126, 192
punishment 2, 40, 48–9, 152

race 1–5, 105, 171, 174
  and criminal justice 116
  and equality 111, 118
radical feminism 124–5, 127
Rand, Ayn 72
Rawls, John 45, 46, 53–65, 69–70, 78, 92–3, 185–6
  and animals 135, 137
  and capitalism 97
  and communitarianism 149–50
  and critics 65–9, 184
  and disability 89–90, 129–30
  and distribution 95
  and equality 113
  and family 126–7
  and global justice 161–2, 163, 165, 176
  and the market 71
reflective equilibrium 55, 65, 192
refugees 170, 171
Regan, Tom 142
relativism 29–30, 192
religion 30, 151
  and Grotius 166
  and Locke 49–50
  and natural law 86
  and persecution 65, 179–80
  and Rawls 63
  see also Islam
Republic (Plato) 10
resource equality 113, 118–19
respect 23, 24
retributive justice 13, 25, 40
Ricardo, David 96
rights 21, 26–30, 34, 40, 72–3, 183
  and equality 110, 112–13, 114
  and Locke 49–50
  and women 38, 125
  see also animal rights; human rights
Robeyns, Ingrid 92
Rollin, Bernard E. 139
Rome Statute 176–7
Roosevelt, Eleanor 27
Rousseau, Jean-Jacques 50–3, 97, 174
rule utilitarianism 35–6

Sandel, Michael 66–7, 101–3, 147, 148, 150
sanitation 156, 157
Saudi Arabia 123
savings 59–60
Scanlon, Thomas 138
Schopenhauer, Arthur 144
Schumpeter, Joseph 96
Schweitzer, Albert 139
segregation 105
self-ownership 72–4
Sen, Amartya 66, 82, 87, 90, 91, 92, 93
  and equality 119
  and global justice 165
  and Rawls 184
Sexual Contract, The (Pateman) 128
Sharia law 123, 152
Singer, Peter 138
slavery 15, 19–20, 44, 73–4, 80, 181
Smith, Adam 96
social contract 46–7, 48–9, 50–2, 92–3, 184, 189
  and animals 137–8
  and disability 131
  and Nozick 73
  and Rawls 53–5, 56–8, 65–6
  and women 67, 126–9
Social Contract, The (Rousseau) 50–2
social democrats 79, 97
social justice 7–9, 108–9, 182–7
social security 84
socialism 62
socio-economic rights 28–9
Socrates 46
Sophocles 8
South Africa 1–5, 27, 30, 61, 186
Sovereign Virtue (Dworkin) 114–15
sovereignty, *see* government
specieism 138
Spheres of Justice (Walzer) 151
state, the, *see* government
subjectivism 192

substantive equality 105
suicide 24, 30
Summa Theologiae (Aquinas) 86
surrogacy 67, 99, 101–2, 103
Sustainable Development Goals (SDGs) 158
Syria 170

taxation 12, 73–4, 80, 104, 117
  and global justice 169
  and immigration 172
Taylor, Charles 149
terrorism 2, 156, 172
Themis 17
Theory of Justice, A (Rawls) 46, 53, 54, 56, 63, 161
  and animals 135
  and co-operation 176
  and critics 68–9
Thirty Years' War 160
Thomas Aquinas, St 86, 136
torture 18, 22, 26, 30
totalitarianism 1–2, 52, 193
trade unions 99
Two Treatises on Government (Locke) 49–50
tyranny 49, 193

unemployment 5, 117, 157
United Nations (UN) 3, 91, 158, 175, 176
  and climate change 173
  and Disability Rights 145
  and FGM 152
  and human rights 27, 28, 155
  and population growth 157
United Nations Children's Emergency Fund (UNICEF) 159
United Nations High Commissioner for Refugees (UNHCR) 170
United States of America (USA) 50, 61, 103, 125, 154
  and equality 105, 107
  and ICC 177
  and race 116
Universal Declaration on Human Rights 26–7, 28
utilitarianism 8, 24, 37, 38–41, 44–5, 193
  and animals 138–9, 145
  and Bentham 34–6, 41–3
  and equality 111–12
  and human rights 29
  and the market 71
  and Nozick 73, 79
  and Rawls 55, 58, 67

veil of ignorance 56, 57, 59, 61, 129–30, 164, 184
Verwoerd, Hendrik 2
Vindication of the Rights of Women, A (Wollstonecraft) 123
violence against women 122, 124, 127, 129
virtue 10, 13–14, 17, 18–19
vivisection 138, 143
volunteerism 102
voting rights 106

Waldron, Jeremy 26
Walzer, Michael 149, 151, 154, 171
war 47, 48, 65, 160
war crimes 176, 177
wealth 5, 6–7, 17, 69–70, 100
  and distribution 71, 72, 73, 74–6, 79
welfare 113, 115
welfare state 62, 79, 104, 172
Westen, Peter 110
Whitehead, Alfred 10
Williams, Sir Bernard 42, 107–8
Wollstonecraft, Mary 123
women 5, 38, 90, 121–9, 145, 165
  and Aristotle 12, 15
  and birth rates 157
  and disability 134
  and equality 111
  and FGM 152
  and social contract 67
  and surrogacy 101–2
  and voting rights 106
working life 122
World Health Organization (WHO) 6, 180
World Trade Organization (WTO) 160

Young, Iris Marion 128